Praise for *The Silent Weaver*

'A wonderfully touching true story of the broken but brilliant Angus MacPhee and the world-class art works he produced while incarcerated in an asylum far from his Hebridean home.'
Michael Russell MSP, *Sunday Herald*

'A fascinating, poignant read.'
Stuart Kelly, *The Scotsman*

'Haunting.'
Colin Waters, *The Herald*

'Like Hutchinson's previous book, the best-selling *Calum's Road*, Angus's tale becomes a way of exploring wider issues – in this case, topics such as art history, the loss of traditional island ways of life and changing attitudes to mental health and care in the community. But the author's deft handling means these points never feel laboured and the result is as moving as it is absorbing. This is a story which will stay with me for a long time and Roger Hutchinson has done his subject proud.'
Morag Lindsay, *Press & Journal*

Leugh mi a' chuid as motha den iomadh eachdraidh-beatha a sgrìobh Roger Hutchinson, *Calum's Road* 'nam measg, agus 'na mo bheachd-sa, se *The Silent Weaver: The Extraordinary Life and Work of Angus MacPhee* as fheàrr air fad . . . Abair leabhar."
Ronald Black, *The Scotsman*

'In much the same way as he did in his book, *Calum's Road*, Roger Hutchinson takes a simple fact story about an isolated individual and gives it the power of myth, providing – what is essentially – local history with a rich universality.'
Donald S. Murray, *Shetland Times*

'A wonderful and illuminating account.'
Donnie Munro, *West Highland Free Press*

Roger Hutchinson is an award-winning author and journalist. After working as an editor in London, in 1977 he joined the *West Highland Free Press* in Skye. Since then he has published fifteen books. He is now a columnist for the *WHFP*, and a book reviewer for *The Scotsman*. His book *The Soap Man* (Birlinn 2003) was shortlisted for the Saltire Scottish Book of the Year (2004) and the bestselling *Calum's Road* (2007) was shortlisted for the Royal Society of Literature's Ondaatje Prize.

THE SILENT WEAVER

*The Extraordinary Life and Work
of Angus MacPhee*

Roger Hutchinson

BIRLINN

First published in 2011 by
Birlinn Limited
West Newington House
10 Newington Road
Edinburgh
EH9 1QS

www.birlinn.co.uk

ISBN: 978 1 84158 971 8

British Library Cataloguing-in-Publication Data
A catalogue record for this book is available from the British Library

Typeset by Edderston Book Design, Peebles
Printed and bound by MBM Print SCS Ltd, Glasgow

MIX
Paper from
responsible sources
FSC® C117931

CONTENTS

PREFACE

The life of Angus MacPhee seems at times more like fiction than fact – it is difficult not to be reminded of the epic Gaelic stories which were still told in his childhood by old men before peat fires over four or five consecutive nights.

A boy from an island far out in the western ocean, who learned antique traditions before riding away on his horse to become a soldier, who experienced a transformational crisis, who then maintained an almost Trappist silence for the rest of his long life while weaving items that nobody understood from the produce of the fields and woods, before burning them. It sounds like a medieval legend, or a flight of fancy better left to a magical realist. In the twentieth century it seems purely fantastic.

But the facts are true. The story of Angus MacPhee wanders down several captivating country lanes. The tenacious old ways of Celtic Britain; the deracination of a remote and insular culture. The under-celebrated adventures of the Lovat Scouts during the Second World War; the drama of remote islanders being sent to garrison islands even more remote than their own. The scandals and achievements of mental health theory and treatment in the second half of the twentieth century; the troublesome and influential realisations of Outsider Art. The possibility of redemption through creativity; the love of family and place . . .

That is the story of a man who was thought to drift through

his own life like an aimless ghost. It is true that Angus MacPhee was robbed of control and direction for a period in his youth. It is also true that he steadily, wilfully won back his character, his substance, and ultimately the place that he loved; the place that for half a century he can only have seen in dreams, but that had inspired the burnt offerings which he made twice a year throughout his adulthood.

One of the many mysteries surrounding Angus MacPhee's handmade filigrees of grass, leaves and flowers is that none of them survive as they originally appeared and few of them survive at all. To a large extent we can only guess at his achievements.

The creations of what must have been his prime between 1946 and 1977 – those fabled patterns of bright green grass and spring blossoms, the gloves and swallow-tailed coats and hats like sunbursts – were all, with the artist's consent if not active cooperation, cremated or composted.

Even those that were saved after 1977 were soon distorted and made colourless by the passing of the seasons. Like classical statuary, or forgotten frescos in the eaves of some Calabrian chapel, their verdant beryls, blues, yellows and reds have all been naturally, inevitably reduced to different shades of brown.

But they impress us even in their deterioration, and that is curious. Are we projecting? Is our imagination allowed too free a rein, so we appreciate not something that actually was, but something as we wish it to have been? Is it a freak show – are we wondering not at the quality of an object, but that it was made at all by a mentally handicapped Gael and former mounted soldier from the Western Isles?

It doesn't matter. During an extraordinary life Angus MacPhee made idiosyncratic objects with unique skills. It is no longer important how we or the critics value them; whether they are described as art, craft or therapy. Their originator was always above and beyond all that, and his weavings have joined him. As he wasted no time giving them marks out of ten, nor need we.

They are in a different place and should be seen from another perspective. The few of his creations that have been preserved are what anthropologists call survivals. They have not only survived from the 1970s and 1980s. They are in essence much older than that. They are living relics of a lost world. They are atavisms. They are like nothing else in twenty-first-century Europe.

They are also symbols of another survival: the endurance, against terrible odds, of the indomitable wit and spirit of Angus MacPhee. That is why we gape.

I would like to thank Angus MacPhee's nephew and niece, Iain Campbell and Eilidh Shaw, for their time and their invaluable help, and Joyce Laing for guiding me patiently through the long story of her own and Angus MacPhee's involvement in Art Extraordinary. Without those three people I could not have written this book. Any errors are of course mine, not theirs.

Neither are errors the fault of any of these men and women... thanks also to Jackie Agnew, Patrick Cockburn, Maggie Cunningham, Wilma Duncan, Shona Grant, George Hendry, Nick Higgins, Brian Johnstone, Iain MacDonald, the late Jimmy 'Apples' Macdonald, Father Michael J. MacDonald, Morag MacDonald, Roddy 'Poker' MacDonald, Alasdair Maceachen, Joan Macintyre, Calum MacKenzie, Chris Mackenzie, Linsey MacKenzie, Tommy MacKenzie, Cailean MacLean, Norman 'Curly' MacLeod, John McNaught, Donald

John MacPherson, Dougie MacPherson, MacTV, Chris Meecham, Mary Miers, Donnie Munro, Rob Polson, Andrew Wiseman and Gus Wylie.

And finally, thanks to Hugh Andrew, Andrew Simmons, Jim Hutcheson, Jan Rutherford and all at Birlinn, to my editor Anita Joseph, and to my agent Stan of Jenny Brown Associates.

Roger Hutchinson
Raasay, 2011

1

THE HORSE SOLDIERS

~ 'Here's to . . . we never have to do it again.' ~

Early in September 1939, riders in battledress cantered down a broad, grassy plain on the western edge of Europe. The young men of Uist were going to war again.

They went in the high hundreds from islands whose populations numbered only a few thousand. Crofting families in the Scottish Hebrides were big families, with a surplus of men in their late teens and twenties to offer to the army and the navy.

Over sixty years later an elderly lady, a sister of one of the men of 1939, would gaze from one end of her small South Uist village to the other. In a still, calm voice she recalled how the girl she had been watched the youths depart from every single croft.

'Two people from that house, somebody from that house,' she said. 'Angus from this house, Father MacQueen's middle brother from that house, two boys from that house . . . They all went the day when war broke out. It was a great adventure for them. They all loved going.'

Some walked to muster, some sailed and some took their horses. The crofters and fishermen of the Outer Hebrides had been for decades willing recruits to the Territorial Army and the Royal Naval Reserve. Drill halls were established in North Uist, Benbecula and South Uist. Teenage boys with few other recreations joined up, learned to parade and do press-ups, and were rewarded by annual excursions to mainland summer camps.

'It was the best way for getting a fortnight's holiday away from the island and enjoying yourselves,' said one Uist man. 'I don't think it was patriotism. For some it might have been, but not as far as I was concerned. The other boys went, and you all went for a fortnight to camp and had a good time.'

Most of those army reservists went from Uist early in September 1939 to be infantrymen in the Cameron Highlanders. But some, a self-consciously select minority, rode off to be horse soldiers with the Lovat Scouts. They were a military anachronism in 1939, but they could not be expected to recognise it. They and their animals were the last representatives of an equestrian culture which had flourished on the greensward of western Uist for millennia.

As they rode to war they skirted mile after mile of ground which their people had turned over for grains and root vegetables using horse-drawn ploughs. They passed over the arenas for popular horse races in the nineteenth and twentieth centuries. They led their mounts through communities which had not yet been colonised by the motor car, the lorry and the tractor.

They rode from all parts of the three distinct islands of North Uist, Benbecula and South Uist. Some districts contributed more horse soldiers than others, by virtue of their greater reliance on horses in everyday crofting life and consequently their superior horsemanship.

One such district was Iochdar at the north end of South Uist. 'The horses in Iochdar were famous throughout the Uists,' said a local priest. 'The Iochdar people have always had the reputation of being "big farmers" and the horses were the most important farm animals. They had to be fed first – every type of croft or farm work depended on them.'

The young Lovat Scouts who rode out of Iochdar on 4 September 1939 included a tall, shy, quietly spoken 24-year-old named Angus Joseph MacPhee – the older brother of that girl who, decades later, would point out one by one the homes of the mobilised men.

Angus and his comrades ignored the main arterial road which ran through the middle of the long island of South Uist. Instead they took their horses – invariably their best and favourite horses – southwards down the machair, along that broad, grassy, westernmost plain, with the Atlantic Ocean surging on their right and the high brown hills of Uist rising on their left, for almost 20 miles until they turned east to the ferry port of Lochboisdale.

Angus MacPhee and the other Lovat Scouts from Iochdar rode proud and erect, in their tunics and their Balmoral bonnets with a diced band, through the busy, familiar townships of the machair. They were almost the only ordinary soldiers from rural Britain to take their horses to the second industrial European war of the twentieth century. They were among the very last active, rather than ceremonial, British horse soldiers.

They were also the only members of the British Army whose horses' bridles were traditionally hand-plaited from coastal marram grass.

The Lovat Scouts had first been raised 40 years earlier by the 14th Lord Lovat, Simon Joseph Fraser, whose extensive hereditary estate encircled Beaufort Castle and the towns of Kiltarlity and Beauly in the eastern Scottish Highlands.

In 1900 Simon Fraser was a 29-year-old former officer in the Queen's Own Cameron Highlanders. He decided to aid his country's war against the Boers in South Africa by assembling a regiment which would utilise the unique rough-country field craft, mettle and clannishness of the Highland estate stalker and ghillie.

The Lovat Scouts had a good Boer War ('half wolf and half jackrabbit', said their American major, Frederick Burnham) and, a few years later, an even better First World War. On the Western Front in 1916 they turned their rifle sights from the stag to the Hun, and formed the British Army's first company of snipers.

In the peace of 1922 the Lovat Scouts were re-formed as a Territorial Army unit with a complement of about 400 soldiers. They were divided into three squadrons. 'A' Squadron recruited from mainland Inverness-shire, and 'C' Squadron from the other northern Highland counties of Sutherland, Ross-shire and Caithness. There was overlap between their geographical constituencies, but the other detachment, 'B' Squadron, was chiefly the Hebridean island unit. 'B' Squadron took men specifically from North Uist, Benbecula, South Uist and Skye, reinforced by some other Gaelic speakers from the western mainland.

Between 1922 and 1939 the Lovat Scouts held 16 summer camps to which the Uist men took their own horses – all but one of them in the mainland Scottish Highlands at such places as Strathpeffer, Nairn and (heavy with folk-memory) Culloden.

Michael Leslie Melville, an officer with the Lovat Scouts between 1936 and 1951 and a historian of the regiment, remembered those pre-war camps with affection. 'It was demanding work and seemed quite "up-to-date",' wrote Melville.

In some of the schemes Major Bill Whitbread, piloting his own aircraft, even represented the Luftwaffe, to the ponies' occasional alarm.

One remembers Sports days with perpetual piping and sunshine, when the highlights were the V.C. race [wherein a horse and jockey would make the outward ride solo, but collect a pillion passenger for the return leg] and inter-Squadron tug-of-war and when old Scouts, some of them very old, came great distances to see the fun.

The officers were kindly invited to the annual Sergeants' Mess Concert and Ceilidh at which the best musical talent in the Regiment was mustered – an evening of inspired fiddle music, piping, Gaelic song and the 'mouth music', with many good tales thrown in.

In 1935 and 1936 the War Office, motivated by ominous events in central Europe, reviewed its regimental functions. It was decided that the Lovat Scouts should be a fully mounted observer regiment of 580 men. Their job would not be that of traditional cavalry, but 'to provide mobile troops for duties of reconnaissance and protection, probably in a minor theatre of war'.

They formed a link between the new world and the old. By the late 1930s the Lovat Scouts, which just 20 years earlier had become the first sharpshooter corps, was the last mounted reconnaissance troop attached to the British Army. The men of the far north and west, who had ridden with Calgacus, Bruce and Wellington, were the ultimate representatives of chivalric warfare from their islands.

In 1933 the 15-year-old Donald John MacPherson of Claddach Baleshare on the west coast machair of North Uist went along to Bayhead Drill Hall and joined the Cameron Highlander Territorials.

'But I was daft about horses,' said Donald John. 'Keen on horses. I loved horses – I used to ride bareback, with my hands waving free. And so four years after I joined I was referred from the Camerons to the Lovat Scouts – with the horses. I only did one camp with the Lovat Scouts, in 1938. There was an awful lot of horses with the Scouts. A lot of men from the islands with horses. We used to have competitions in the camp – horse races and the like.'

Angus MacPhee of Iochdar, who was also daft about horses, was enlisted in 1934 to the Lovat Scouts Territorial Army unit at Carnan Drill Hall, a couple of miles east of his home.

In peacetime, both men were accustomed to equipping their precious ponies with bridles and other accoutrements expertly woven from the thick, strong strands of marram grass which proliferated on the dunes of western Uist.

'We used marram grass horses' collars,' said Donald John MacPherson. 'We never made them, but we bought them from Neil MacVicar in Baleshare. He made horses' collars for pulling the cart from marram grass. MacVicar's family, his boys, used to make them and sell them in the district.'

In Iochdar, Angus MacPhee did not have to buy woven marram grass. He had known how to make it since boyhood. 'In the '30s and the '20s they could weave with grass,' said Angus's sister Peigi, 'they could weave with heather, and they could make the marram grass . . . that's what the old houses were all thatched with, that's what my father would thatch with.'

As August turned into September in 1939 the lives of Angus MacPhee and Donald John MacPherson, which had been connected hitherto by the same Gaelic language and culture, Hebridean lifestyle and military affiliation, but separated by two tidal strands and the small island of Benbecula, converged beneath the clouds of a late summer war.

On Thursday 31 August the British fleet mobilised and the men of the Royal Naval Reserve were called up. The next day, Friday 1 September, Nazi Germany invaded Poland, to whom the United Kingdom was bound by treaty.

'That Friday night,' said Donald John MacPherson, 'I was as usual in my bed, reading a book, and a knock came to the door at one o'clock in the morning. It was them calling us out, to be at Bayhead Drill Hall the next day, Saturday morning at eleven o' clock. We were told then that on Monday we were going away. We got our uniforms from the drill hall, went back and got the horse.'

On Saturday 2 September, as Donald John MacPherson and Angus MacPhee were collecting their uniforms and instructions from Bayhead and Carnan drill halls in North Uist and South Uist respectively, compulsory military service for all British men between the ages of 18 and 41 was announced.

On Sunday 3 September 1939, as the two Uist men were attending their last church services at home for a very long time, Prime Minister Neville Chamberlain declared war on Germany.

Donald John MacPherson's courageous Second World War lasted until 1945 and would take him across two continents.

Angus MacPhee was beginning an uncharted journey which would occupy the remainder of his long life. Donald John went to North America and southern Europe, and returned alive to tell the tales. Angus went to unmapped places, in which he had to create his own means of expression and realise a lonely, simple and precious form of solace. He would never properly return.

Over 100 Lovat Scouts left North Uist, Benbecula and South Uist on Monday 4 September. Donald John MacPherson put on his uniform and mounted his 'lovely' mare Jessie. A few hundred yards up the track from their family house his sister Morag took his photograph. Then he rode east to the North Uist pier at Lochmaddy, took a steamer with the other 30 North Uist members of 'B' Company to the mainland railhead at Kyle of Lochalsh, and both Jessie and Donald John were transported by train from Kyle to the Lovat Scouts' muster at Beauly, a small market town north-west of Inverness.

Further south in Benbecula somebody had the bright idea of mustering the local unit in the back yard of a celebrated howff called the Creagorry Inn. Lieutenant Simon MacDonald had been sent from the mainland by way of Skye on a fishing boat to shepherd the Uist section of 'B' Company safely to Beauly. The young officer arrived at Creagorry and 'spent what seemed like hours exhorting, pleading and eventually driving troopers out of the ever-open bar ... Then the minister [probably, in that island at that time, a Roman Catholic priest] had a word with each man and finally we got separated from the weeping female attachments, and rode forth bravely into the waters of the ford [to South Uist] ... The scene was not unmoving, the pipes playing, relatives waving from the shore and the horses splashing through the water.'

In Iochdar that morning, Angus MacPhee sat in uniform, his kit slung over his saddle and a cigarette hanging rakishly from the corner of his mouth, astride what he would later describe as 'a fine gelding'. One of his sisters took his photograph. Then he rode south with his friends, up the South Uist machair to Lochboisdale. Those who could do so took their own mounts. Those who could not borrowed horses from other crofters and then sold them to the army, posting the money back to the original owners.

The late summer weather had been deteriorating ever since the declaration of war. Low cloud obscured the hills, and the watercourses which ran from the east into the western ocean were swollen by heavy rain. Seven miles south of Iochdar the horses and riders had trouble crossing the burn which ran at full spate through the township of Howmore. They were regaled on their journey by a veteran of the First World War, Farrier Sergeant MacRury of Benbecula, telling his fellow Scouts of a telegram he had supposedly received that very morning. 'How much to remain neutral?' Sergeant MacRury's message had read. 'Signed, Hitler.' MacRury's reply was uncompromising. 'Nothing doing,' he signalled Berlin. 'We'll fight it out same as last time! Signed, MacRury.'

South of Howmore, the high walls of Stoneybridge School rose out of the mist like a fortress. They gathered their ponies inside the school's stone walls, lit a fire in the schoolroom, were given 'a splendid evening meal' by Stoneybridge women, and settled down for the night.

At about 9.30 p.m. a terrific thunderstorm erupted and many of the 70 ponies broke loose. The Scouts dashed outside and spent 'a couple of soggy hours catching them and re-wiring them by the light of the lightning'. The storm passed and gave way to black night. At a dawn parade all the ponies were miraculously discovered still to be present at Stoneybridge School, but one was dead. A Court of Inquiry later determined that it had been struck by lightning. Lieutenant Simon MacDonald notified the police and asked them to dispose of the body. He took the horse's blanket, headcollar and surcingle on south, with his surviving 'damp but cheerful band' augmented by Lovat Scouts Territorials from the villages of the middle and south of Uist, to Lochboisdale.

At Lochboisdale pier, while Simon MacDonald was signing receipts for some 80 ponies, his soldiers repaired to the adjacent Lochboisdale Hotel for a final dram. To the lieutenant's great relief the hotel's proprietor, a future captain of the local Home Guard named Finlay Mackenzie, voluntarily closed his own bar until the soldiers' boat sailed. It left the deep sheltered harbour of Loch Boisdale with bagpipes wailing from the decks and darkness falling, and immediately ran into another tremendous storm.

They were embarked on a MacBrayne's passenger and goods steamer which had been requisitioned for their sea crossing to Kyle of Lochalsh. On that second full night of the Second World War the ship sailed with no lights showing, across the Minch through a strong, gusting wind and driving rain. She steered westerly past the Small Isles of Canna, Rum and Eigg, up the Sound of Sleat and through the Kylerhea narrows. From Kyle, they too were taken by train to join the MacRaes and MacKenzies and Frasers of the Highland glens at the great muster in Beauly.

In the first week of the war almost 500 Lovat Scouts congregated in Beauly from all corners of the north of Scotland. The islanders of 'B' Squadron were quartered at the Beaufort Home Farm, in what Donald John MacPherson described as 'a big shed'. Another member of 'B' Squadron, Donald John MacKenzie from Kintail, said that on the farm 'chaos ruled mainly'.

> We slept in the byre on the concrete floor with three blankets, straw palliasse and pillow and boy was it cold and hard. We had some soup and stew to eat out of tin bowls and plates which when washed were stacked on the trestle tables in the open. When you went for breakfast in the morning they were stuck together by rust having not been dried. A couple of warmer days later we either picked the maggots out of those bowls and tins or did without any food.
>
> We had billet guard and picket on horse-lines to do. The ponies were tied six feet apart to a rope stretched between two strainers and heel stops on one rear leg and a pin hammered into the ground to keep them from turning round and kicking each other to bits. Those on guard when off duty slept under the belt for driving the threshing mill and often the rats slid down the belt and jumped off to land on a sleeping body.
>
> One chap who had some grease spilt on his puttees (we wore puttees, britches and spurs) had the strap of his puttee eaten clean through by a rat. We eventually got good at killing them with our bayonets.

At first they kept their horses and stayed in the Highlands. Second Lieutenant Michael Leslie Melville remembered that during the winter of 1939–40, 'Training was carried out in riding and horse-management, drill both mounted and on foot, weapon-training and shooting, spying and observation, map-reading and compass work, signalling and reporting, night training, anti-gas precautions . . .'

'Our main task for the first period of time,' said Donald

John MacKenzie, 'was looking after and training the ponies, being kitted out with saddles and fighting equipment'.

> We trained in front of Beaufort Castle on the ponies. They went round in a wide circle and on command we slid off the tail end of our ponies and jogged by the side of the following one for a bit and then sprang off the ground on to the pony's back and this went on for some time. Included in the scheme was sitting back to front, sideways, on our backs, on our bellies on the back of the ponies, always with the pony trotting in a circle. For the first while we were very stiff and sore all over, especially our posteriors as we spent hours in the saddle or bareback, but soon we were very competent riders.

One squadron swam its ponies across the River Beauly in midwinter spate. Another rode through the county seat of Dingwall wearing gas masks, prompting a letter to the *Ross-shire Journal* which wondered why their horses had no such protection. They played football and shinty and badminton, and were entertained by Sir Harry Lauder. They were sometimes allowed rough game shooting, and when they were not they poached pheasant. The Lovat Scouts was a largely Gaelic-speaking regiment, and in 'B' Squadron little else was heard. At that time over 90 per cent of the Uist population spoke Gaelic as a native first language, and roughly 30 per cent spoke no English. The islanders' non-commissioned officers usually gave instructions and orders in Gaelic, introducing such terms as 'Bren gun' and 'respirator' to its vocabulary.

They were given a thorough medical inspection. Fifteen Scouts were discharged as unfit for service, and another 21 were limited to Home Service. Those 36 men did not include Trooper Angus MacPhee from Iochdar.

After seven months spent training in the hills and glens of

the eastern Highlands, early in April 1940 the Lovat Scouts were sent to stables and billets near Sutton-on-Trent in the English Midlands. The Hebrideans and the horses of 'B' Squadron entrained at Beauly Station. The population of the town turned out to wave them off, and to hear the strains of their pipes disappear quickly down the track to Inverness, the Scottish Lowlands and the south.

The truth was that by the spring of 1940, the British Army did not know what to do with its mounted Highland soldiers and their garron ponies. The war had not turned out as might have been anticipated in 1936. The Lovat Scouts' deployment to 'a minor theatre of war', which had been mooted four years earlier, no longer seemed practical. 'A minor theatre of war' had probably suggested some distant, trackless part of the British Empire which required policing.

In April 1940 any such ambition was almost redundant. The conflict seemed likely to be a battle of survival for the two main Allies, Britain and France. The Soviet Union and Nazi Germany had signed a non-aggression pact and carved up Poland. Fascist Italy had thrown in her lot with the German Axis. Finland was engaged and neutralised by the Soviets. Adolf Hitler clearly had his eye on the other militarily vulnerable nations of Scandinavia and the Low Countries as well as France. If they all fell – as they would – the archipelago of islands which comprised the United Kingdom would be isolated and effectively surrounded.

In such interesting times the Lovat Scouts arrived in Nottinghamshire. Their commanding officers had tried to get them posted across the Channel to help with the defence of France, but it was decided that 'the flat country of Flanders can hardly be considered the ideal terrain for the employment of the Lovat Scouts'. Some mention was made of Palestine, where the army's residual equine – rather than mechanised – cavalry regiments were already deployed, but as quickly forgotten.

Instead, Angus MacPhee, Donald John MacPherson, Donald John MacKenzie and most of the rest of 'B' Squadron found themselves getting off a train at Sutton-on-Trent on 6 April 1940 and making their way to civilian billets in such manorial English hamlets as Kelham and East Markham. They were in fact just 30 miles from Derby, where almost exactly 200 years earlier those of their ancestors who had ridden with Charles Edward Stuart had camped before being ordered to abandon their assault on London and march back to the Highlands.

'We had a feather bed in which one sank almost out of sight and was very warm,' said Donald John MacKenzie of the Highlanders' return visit in 1940, unconsciously reiterating the sentiments of Jacobite officers in December of 1745. 'The food was pretty grim, a piece of toast and one sausage or one egg for breakfast. The man of the house was a small elderly chap who never spoke to us, played darts most of the time so much so that he had almost gone through his dart board at the twenty and the bull.'

Three days later, on 9 April 1940, Germany invaded Denmark and Norway, the two nations which guarded the Skagerrak, the straits leading out of the Baltic Sea, and whose 1,200-mile western flanks opened directly onto the North Atlantic Ocean from the Arctic Circle to Heligoland. British troops were sent to assist the Norwegian resistance. On 19 April, as a scarcely noticed precautionary measure, a small detachment of Royal Marines was landed in the Faroe Islands, a remote Danish property halfway between the Shetland Islands, which were already garrisoned by British forces, and Iceland, which soon would be.

On 22 April, the Lovat Scouts ceased to be the last mounted reconnaissance unit in the British Army. They were ordered to hand over their ponies to the army's Remount Department. Most of the horses left on cattle trucks to the Remount Depot at Melton Mowbray in Leicestershire – 'to the butchers, I think', said Donald John MacPherson, although Michael Leslie Melville said that the War Office used them firstly as pack-ponies and then honoured a request made by the regiment 'that when the ponies were no longer required for army use, they should be returned to the Highlands for sale'.

Angus MacPhee's 'fine gelding' had a happier fate. He sold it to an admiring officer. But after the third week in April 1940, none of 'B' Squadron would ever again ride the pony which had accompanied him from a croft in the Hebrides on that thundery day in September 1939. Henceforth they would be infantry foot-soldiers.

They were unsentimental. 'We were mechanised and given transport of all descriptions,' said Donald John MacKenzie. 'We still had to do a route march each week, and as we still wore our puttees, breeches and spurs, and the weather got hotter, and worst of all my boots, one pair, were getting too small for me . . . We suffered . . .'

With the British Army, Navy and Air Force still giving some assistance to the Norwegian resistance, most of the Lovat Scouts expected to be sent to Scandinavia. For a short time, the War Office planned to send them there. On 1 May an advance party of one troop of 'B' Squadron under Lieutenant Simon MacDonald left Nottinghamshire in a convoy of lorries for

Greenock on Clydeside, probably to prepare for passage to Norway. But Oslo fell to the Germans and most of the British Army withdrew on 2 May, leaving behind a small expeditionary corps in the far north of the country. Eight days later the *Wehrmacht* invaded Belgium, Holland and Luxembourg.

For three weeks the Lovat Scouts were divided. They stood-to 250 miles apart, in Greenock and rural Nottinghamshire, while at home and abroad matters moved with bewildering speed. On 11 May Winston Churchill replaced Neville Chamberlain as Prime Minister and a national government was formed. The Low Countries tottered and fell. On 21 May, with Holland and Belgium as well as almost all of Norway and Denmark in German hands, the rest of the Lovat Scouts were put on a train from England to Glasgow. They joined their advance troop, who had, in Donald John MacKenzie's words, 'idled about there in Greenock'.

On 23 May 1940 the Lovat Scouts embarked on the transatlantic liner *Ulster Prince* and, with an escort of two destroyers, steamed southwards out of the Clyde. They left behind, considered unfit for active service or suitable only for Home Detail, a total of 103 men, who did not include Trooper Angus MacPhee.

The small flotilla rounded the Mull of Kintyre and sailed north into the Minch. To starboard the Skyemen and western Highlanders 'could see the hills of Skye and home'. To port, the *Uibhistich* gazed upon Beinn Mhòr, Hecla, Eaval and the other stony heights of eastern Uist until they disappeared from view.

Most of the ordinary troopers aboard the *Ulster Prince* still thought that they were heading for Norway. They were designated part of the North West Expeditionary Force, the same title given to the body of men that had, in the sub-Arctic region of Narvik, in alliance with Norwegian, French and Polish battalions, achieved a measure of success against the Germans. But as the *Ulster Prince* left port, the new British government was privately agreeing to end its calamitous Norwegian campaign by abandoning the place, and to reinforce its own sea power by occupying other North Atlantic landfalls. So having cleared the Butt of Lewis at the northernmost tip of the Outer Hebrides, instead of setting a north-easterly course to Scandinavia, the *Ulster Prince* continued due north.

Early in the morning of 25 May 1940, Angus MacPhee, Donald John MacPherson, Donald John MacKenzie and 477 other Lovat Scouts sailed through a thick mist into Torshavn, the capital town of the Faroe Islands.

Sending them to the Faroes made sense to the War Office, if not to the Lovat Scouts. Almost 500 hillsmen and islanders from the remotest parts of northern Britain were told to garrison a group of remote, hilly, northern islands. By British military standards, it was good casting.

Tactically, the annexation of the Faroes and then Iceland by Britain meant that while the German fleet could dock on almost the whole of the Atlantic seaboard of mainland Europe, the Royal Navy still commanded the ocean itself. The garrisons were symbolic as well as practical. Along with Iceland and the Shetland group, those islands represented castles of occupation on a hostile sea.

A fellow soldier, the ornithologist and author Kenneth Williamson, would later describe what Angus MacPhee saw when he looked over the rail at Torshavn on that May morning. 'Round about the town,' wrote Williamson, who arrived in the Faroes the following year to operate the military library there, 'the hills were a watery green, rock-scarred and boulder-strewn, and seared with trickling rills.'

> They rose in dreary, inhospitable slopes that looked devoid of interest or charm, rearing steeply to jagged crests of broken rock and scree beyond which one could imagine a great stony plateau ranging away for mile after mile.
>
> The monotony of the surroundings cast into bold relief the attractiveness of this tiny, compact town spreading over the lowest slopes towards the water's edge ... Time after time as the troopship lay outside the harbour, waiting for the berth to clear, the many-coloured town was almost blotted out, or appeared dimly to view, like pieces of a shattered rainbow thrown into confusion behind the lurking cloud.
>
> The buildings crowded together with disdain for pattern, plan or uniformity of any kind. There were all shapes and sizes and kinds of buildings clinging to the knolls and shreds of fields, their roofs and walls shining with the wetness, glowing with a gay medley of colours ...
>
> Here bricks and mortar and slated roofs are practically unknown ... The narrow, often hilly streets; the simple, unadorned frontages; the long grass growing profusely on the roofs; the liberal use of bright paints that shine through the damp mists, or of darker hues that draw back like shadows in contrast – all of these so enliven every change of scene that one cannot but marvel at the inspiration which so obviously dwells in the shelter of those hopeless-looking hills.

As the *Ulster Prince* docked at the pier with its Uist pipers playing aboard, and the Lovat Scouts disembarked, 'crowds of people including hundreds of children, came down from the town to look on and remained there all day'.

In 1940 there were 30,000 Faroese living on 18 of their 20 islands. Three thousand of them resided in Torshavn; the rest were scattered between fishing villages and placid agricultural settlements. Apart from the fact that the Faroes were dry islands with no public bars or other licensed premises – beer and spirits were imported for the troops with their other rations – it was an easy community for Hebrideans and Highlanders to understand. Both the Faroes and the Western Isles of Scotland had once been the homes of eremitic monks from the Celtic Church; both had been part of the Kingdom of Norway (the Western Isles until 1266, the Faroes until 1814); both were accustomed to being governed in modern times from capital cities (London and Copenhagen) which did not speak their languages (Gaelic and a derivation of Old Norse). The Faroese, a sea-faring people, were well aware that their nearest neighbours lived in the Scottish islands, less than 200 miles away, and that the Faroes were considerably closer to Aberdeen, Dundee and Glasgow than to Reykjavik or Copenhagen.

Whatever their historical connections, remote communities develop similar courtesies. By and large the Lovat Scouts were made as welcome in the Faroes as Faroese soldiers in similar circumstances would have been hosted in the Uists. There were tensions during the occupation. There was a minority of German sympathisers among the Faroese. There were also Faroese separatists who resented British cooperation with Danish officials in exile, and the fact that Winston Churchill had announced that when Germany was defeated the Faroe Islands 'will be handed back to Denmark'. There were Faroese who objected to the steady stream of young women made pregnant by British soldiers. There was occasional robbery from army stores; there were strikes for better pay for Faroese civilians employed by the British military. But on the whole . . .

'Oh, we had a great reception,' said Donald John MacPherson. 'They invited us into their homes. And you know, they had all sorts of things that weren't in the Western Islands. They had telephones, and electricity – things we didn't have. And they were friendly, oh, very, very friendly.'

'The Faroese are hospitable and kindly people,' reported the British novelist Eric Linklater, who, because of his family's Shetland connections, was asked by the Ministry of Information in 1941 to prepare a booklet entitled *The Northern Garrisons*.

> Very soon after the occupation they opened their houses to our soldiers, who now, except the incurably shy, have all a modest circle of acquaintances. Their hospitality mollifies one of the routine duties of the Lovat Scouts: the patrolling, that is, of hill-top paths and hidden fjords, of tiny hamlets under a mountainside, and almost inaccessible beaches. Some of their patrols are short, a few hours' marching, but others are three-day tours, and on these they must make their own bivouacs, do their own field-cooking. But whenever they come to a village, someone is almost sure to ask them in for cakes and coffee.

The Lovat Scouts were in the Faroes to stop the Germans being there. Their duties were concentrated on that mission. The Germans made no serious attempt to invade the islands, by air or by sea, but the Luftwaffe regularly attacked the land bases and military and civilian shipping by strafing, bombs and torpedo-planes.

'We took over from a detachment of Royal Marines who were guarding the main installations,' said Donald John MacKenzie.

> Radio station, Fort Skansin [a small sixteenth-century redoubt overlooking Torshavn, which became the Royal Navy's Command Headquarters], pier, marine cable tele-

phone station. We were billeted in the main hall and other halls in the town and the regiment was soon dispersed on the major islands throughout the Faroes – of which there are 17 altogether.

As each squadron was moved about the islands in rotation to provide guards on certain strategic points, we were moved by boat. Sometimes it was on the *Suigrill*, the regular mail boat which took us especially to the larger islands, which was on her regular route. Other times we went by the *Poppy*, a 48- to 50-foot Norwegian fishing boat which had come over to Faroe some time earlier to escape the Nazis and was commandeered by the British. The chap in charge of her was John MacIsaac from Benbecula – she was crewed by Scouts and was a very sea-worthy craft.

Many Allied ships were attacked. Faroese fishing boats were obliged to display their national colours so that Allied vessels and aeroplanes knew who they were, and they took the brunt of the German assault. The islands lost almost 200 men at sea during the war, which was slightly more than the number of Faroese women – 151 – who married British soldiers. In the credit column, the Lovat Scouts brought down a German Heinkel bomber with concerted Bren gun fire. Its pilot survived, to confess that he had mistaken the Bren gun fire for anti-aircraft flak. ('When held firm,' a Second World War veteran recalled, '[a Bren gun] was accurate enough to punch a hole in a brick wall with a single magazine.')

In terms of casualties the Germans won the Battle of the Faroes. But they never set foot on Faroese soil unless as prisoners, so the home side won the war.

The Lovat Scouts were in the Faroe Islands virtually without relief for two years. They played inter-squadron football matches. They had their pictures taken in full rig at the studio of the Torshavn photographer. The regimental pipe band, which was comprised entirely of Uistmen such as Donald John MacPherson, also practised on the 'hard grit' Torshavn football pitch. They ate tinned army rations – featuring the green cans of Maconochie's Irish beef stew which sustained British troops through both of the major twentieth-century conflicts – relieved occasionally by edible gifts from the Faroese. They received mail from home three weeks or a month after it had been posted.

And they patrolled, and patrolled, and patrolled. One stormy winter's night Lieutenant Sir Simon Campbell-Orde took a detachment from North Uist on an 18-mile coastal patrol which proved so arduous that on return they were granted a rum ration. Sir Simon raised his tin mug and asked his men who or what they would like to toast. 'Here's to . . .' said a voice from the ranks, 'we never have to do it again.'

'B' Squadron's commanding officer, said Donald John MacKenzie,

> was Major Richard Fleming and he was a fitness fanatic, as they say nowadays. We used to go on long route marches, sometimes in full service marching orders which included our large pack and sometimes in battle order which meant as before with the exception of the big pack.
>
> One day in Tvøroyri he took us on a seven-mile route march round the end of a long fjord, and when we had reached our destination we were made to strip off all our clothes and working in pairs made a package of all our clothes, equipment and rifles, all inside our gas capes. The complete thing was about four feet long and fifteen inches wide and a foot deep.
>
> When tied securely and done properly it floated. We were then ordered into the sea, by this time shivering with

cold and apprehension, wondering if our package would really float, leak or sink. He grabbed our package, placed a Bren gun on top and swam a considerable distance to prove it worked.

As most of us could not swim at that time, we did not venture out of our depth but got ourselves wet just the same. After a few minutes the Major came ashore and shouted, 'Three minutes to dress and line up on the road.' Our biggest difficulty was to dry our bodies, dry enough to get our clothes on in such a short time, but we need not have worried as some of our packs were not too waterproof, including the Major's ...

There is nothing as difficult as trying to get a wet body into dry clothes or even socks. We were lined up on the road and marched off with the Major in front. When we had marched a couple of hundred yards, we were given the order to double and another couple of hundred yards to march and so it went on as a forced march for seven miles back to the billets.

'It was a great pleasure to see one of their squadrons playing a war game,' wrote Major Eric Linklater, 'attacking over a wide valley, for the scouts who first advanced had been stalkers on one of the great deer forests, and they moved with the speed and economy, the expert ease of professionals. And the troopers following them went swiftly and with confidence, for they knew that sort of ground very well indeed – rough moorland, peat-bog, and grey boulders – and could find without delay the paths that would take them forward, yet keep them under cover. It was incongruous, of course, but none the less impressive, to see a pair of highly respectable gillies walking-up their game with Tommy-guns.'

Such was the life in 1940, 1941 and 1942 of Donald John MacPherson, Donald John MacKenzie and hundreds of other

Lovat Scouts. MacPherson and MacKenzie were relieved on the Faroes by the 12th Cameronians in June 1942. They sailed out of Torshavn fjord on a late, light northern night with their Uist pipe band playing 'Happy we've been a' thegither'.

Back in Scotland they were sent to guard the Royal Family during its six-week summer holiday at Balmoral Castle. They trained in the Grampians and Cairngorms. At the end of 1943 they sailed on the *Mauretania* from Liverpool to New York, where at least one Uist serviceman enjoyed a cheerful rendezvous with Hebridean emigrants. They travelled from there to the Canadian Rocky Mountains, where they were re-trained once again, this time as a skiing Mountaineer Regiment. In April 1944 the refreshed and newly skilled Lovat Scouts took a train from the Rockies to the North Atlantic port of Halifax, Nova Scotia. In a Halifax barber's shop an officer of 'B' Squadron overheard some local civilians talking in an unfamiliar dialect of his native language. 'When were you last in the Highlands?' he asked them, in Gaelic. 'Three generations ago,' replied the emigrants, in Gaelic.

In July 1944 they landed in Naples. As the hot and bloody summer turned into autumn and winter, and as 1944 turned into 1945, they fought their way up the Italian peninsula. When Germany surrendered on 4 May 1945, Donald John MacPherson, Donald John MacKenzie and the other Lovat Scouts were still fighting. In the nine-month course of their Italian campaign the regiment took many losses and achieved many victories. They were awarded three Military Crosses, a George Medal, a Distinguished Conduct Medal, seven Military Medals and three British Empire Medals. Thirty-six of their small number were mentioned in despatches. All of them won the Italian Star.

But Angus MacPhee of 'B' Squadron, Trooper MacPhee of Iochdar in South Uist, was no longer with them. He had left his friends behind. His health, which had been robust in the eastern Highlands and the English Midlands, collapsed on the Faroe Islands. Thereafter his experiences were in another world.

In the Faroes Angus MacPhee slid helplessly and inexorably into a condition which his comrades and commanding officers would identify only as catatonia. He became uncommunicative, then worse than uncommunicative. Not only would he not obey orders; he would appear not to have heard them. He became incapable of soldierly duties and of everyday self-care. Neither the medic nor the Roman Catholic padre could halt his decline, let alone reverse it. To veterans of the First World War, it would have seemed that Angus MacPhee was afflicted by shell-shock without having been shelled.

It was not easily understood. His officers noted that Trooper MacPhee had been involved in no recorded cases of drunkenness. His military conduct had, before his arrival in the Faroes, been very good. He had the sheet of an honest and sober soldier.

A theatre of war was no place for diagnosis or treatment. On Christmas Eve, 24 December 1940, after exactly seven months in the Faroe Islands, Angus MacPhee was put on a relief vessel and shipped with the outgoing mail to Leith, the port of the city of Edinburgh.

2

TIR A' MHURAIN

~ *'The houseman is twisting twigs of heather into ropes to hold down thatch, a neighbour crofter is twining quicken roots into cords to tie cows, while another is plaiting bent grass into baskets to hold meal.'* ~

Angus MacPhee was born in 1915 in Nettlehole, a tiny village in the central belt of Scotland 14 miles due east of Glasgow.

His father worked as a ploughman. Neil MacPhee had left his native South Uist almost three decades earlier to seek employment on the mainland. Neil was born in 1861 in the township of Balgarva in the district of Iochdar.

Neil MacPhee was the youngest child in a large family, whose mother died when he was an infant. His father Angus was 45 years old when Neil was born, and Neil's oldest brother Francis was his senior by 18 years.

The MacPhees of Balgarva described themselves as tenant farmers for most of the nineteenth century. They were tenants-at-will of the landowner, who was firstly the bankrupt hereditary laird Macdonald of Clanranald, then the wealthy property speculator Colonel John Gordon of Aberdeenshire, then the colonel's son, and finally the colonel's son's widow, Lady Emily Gordon Cathcart of Berkshire. They had no security of tenure until 1886, when the Crofters' Act made them safe from summary eviction. Thereafter, old Angus MacPhee and his sons called themselves what they had actually been for a hundred years or more: crofters.

Their croft, old Angus's croft at lot number 52 Balgarva, could be inherited by one man only. That was certain to be Francis, who in middle age was still single and helping his elderly father to work the rough land. So in his twenties Neil MacPhee went south to Lochboisdale and made the long ferry crossing from South Uist to Oban on the western seaboard of Argyllshire in search of work.

The reasons for his departure were commonplace. In May 1883, when Neil was 22 years old, Father Donald MacColl of Iochdar drew a grim portrait of his district to a government commission which was sitting across the strand in Benbecula. Crofters such as the MacPhees were, said the priest, rack-rented for poor land upon which they had no security of tenure. 'The best arable and grazing lands are in the hands of the tacksmen [tenants of comparatively large farms], and at a low rent. Crofters have been sent to inferior lands . . .'

Iochdar was also, in the 1880s, overpopulated by poor landless cottars who had moved onto the common grazings and the moorland there 'from all quarters of the country' – from elsewhere in South Uist, from North Uist and Benbecula, and even from the distant islands of Tiree and Skye. 'We are yearly getting poorer,' said Father MacColl. 'We are hemmed in on all sides. Deprived of the common, we are confined to our original crofts, and yearly plough the same exhausted and unproductive ground . . .'

In 1891 Neil MacPhee was employed as an agricultural labourer and living in lodgings on Oban's High Street. His landlord and landlady were Donald and Jessie Currie, an Iochdar couple of his generation who had also emigrated from their 'exhausted and unproductive ground' to live and work on the mainland.

At that juncture Neil was 30 years old, single and spoke only Gaelic. His schooling in South Uist had clearly been perfunctory and had equally clearly not fully educated him in English, which was in 1891 already the default language of most of the Oban conurbation. He would have got by. More than half of the population of the town spoke Gaelic as well as English, and in the surrounding countryside – where he would have laboured – the proportion of Gaelic speakers was much higher. But if Neil MacPhee was to travel any further south and east, he would need to acquire an English vocabulary. It is likely that he was helped with this in the house on the High Street. Donald and Jessie Currie and their young sons, all three of whom had been born in Oban, spoke both Gaelic and English.

For the next three decades Neil MacPhee had the life of an itinerant farm labourer on the Scottish mainland. His life was itinerant by definition rather than choice. Farmhands were hired at town fairs at Whitsuntide, seven weeks after Easter, and at Michaelmas in late September. The terms of hire were usually for six months or a year. Deals were struck verbally, and cemented by employers handing over a small downpayment called airles money. Once they had accepted airles money, labourers were legally bound to honour the agreement.

'A skilled, unmarried farmworker's wages,' wrote John

Lorne Campbell, 'were then [in the 1890s] about fourteen to eighteen pounds [roughly £840 to £1,080 in the early twenty-first century] for the half-year, plus lodgings in a bothy, that is, an outside building near the farm, where the accommodation might consist of a bedroom and a kitchen, with no water laid on, and, of course, no indoor sanitation. Oatmeal, milk, potatoes and coal were provided by the employer, and the workers were expected to do their own cooking... pay in the old days was in real gold sovereigns that would keep their value, and tobacco cost only threepence-halfpence [90 pence] an ounce and whisky three and sixpence [£10.50] a bottle...'

Agricultural hiring fairs were an almost undiluted legacy of the Middle Ages. But although the employers obviously had the whiphand, and some drove a harsher bargain than others, and the system was often brutal to elderly and infirm labourers, hiring fairs were not exactly slave auctions. In the small world of Scottish regional agriculture, farmers and labourers often knew and even liked and respected each other. Healthy, strong and experienced workers also learned to play the market without sentiment, and to set employers against one another.

Many Western Isles men of Neil MacPhee's generation crossed the Minch to Scotland for similar work. One of them, Angus MacLellan of Loch Eynort in South Uist, left an account of a hiring fair at Aberfeldy in western Perthshire which probably took place at Michaelmas 1894.

MacLellan had left South Uist, where 'there was no work to be had', in 1889, at around the same time as Neil MacPhee. After working a two-year term on the farm at Tirinie, near Blair Atholl, he told his master Robert Menzies that he would not re-engage as he was going home to Uist. Menzies approved of the islander's domestic instincts and wished him well. The

25-year-old Angus MacLellan walked away from Tirinie and instead of returning to the Hebrides promptly travelled 12 miles south to Aberfeldy fair.

'There was a lad from Uist out there,' he remembered almost 70 years later, 'and he met me in the town, and asked me if I had been hired.'

'I've not,' I said, 'I haven't been hired yet.'

'Do you want a place?' he asked.

'I do,' I said.

'Well,' he said, 'a man was speaking to me down there just now, to see if I could get a secondman [a ploughman's assistant] for him.'

'Where's he at?' I asked.

'Beside Loch Tummel.'

'Is it a good place?'

'It is indeed,' he said. 'I spent three years working for him.'

Well, you could only get a year's engagement [at Aberfeldy that Michaelmas], engagements of six months weren't going at all.

'Oh well, if you spent three years there,' I said, 'I think I might spend one. Is he a good master?'

'Oh yes, indeed. Come along, then, I've only just left the boss here.'

We went along; the farmer met us just at the square.

'Here's a lad for you,' said the Uistman, 'who hasn't found a place yet.'

'Oh, very good,' said the farmer – Thomas MacDonald was his name – 'very good. Are you working here already?'

'I am,' I said. 'I'm working at Tirinie.'

'Oh aye. Is it there you are?'

'It is,' I said.

'How long is it since you came there?'

'It's more than two years,' I said.

'Oh indeed then, it's likely you'll be fit enough for me. It's a secondman I'm needing. What wages do you want?'

'I'll need to get sixteen pounds or fifteen pounds [for six months] anyway,' I said.

'Ah, well,' he said, 'wages are down this year. No one's getting more than fifteen pounds. But I'll give you thirteen.'

'Oh, that won't do,' I said.

'Oh, well there isn't so much work to do for me as there is at Tirinie at all. I know Tirinie very well.'

'Well, I'm sure it isn't to be taking my ease that you want me for. How many acres have you in every break?'

'About twenty.'

'And you've only two pairs of horses?'

'Yes.'

'Well, I'm sure there'll be plenty of work there itself . . .'

'Well,' said Thomas, 'you'll get fourteen pounds, then, and your lodging free above that.'

'Oh, very good,' I said.

He went and put his hand in his pocket then and gave me a crown as airles money. Then he went to see Robert Menzies, my boss.

'I've just engaged one of your lads,' he said to him.

'Oh, have you?' said Robert. 'Which one of them have you got?'

'Angus MacLellan.'

'Aye? I didn't think that fellow was going to engage today at all . . .'

The next day Robert Menzies came where I was working.

'So,' he said, 'did you engage at the fair?'

'Well, I did, but I didn't expect to at all when I left the house.'

'Well, then,' he said, 'it's best for you to stay where you are, and I'll send him – what did he give you as airles money?'

'He gave me a crown.'

'I'll send it to him myself, then, if you'll stay where you are.'

'Do you want to send me to prison?' I asked.

'He won't do anything to you if you stay where you are,' he said. 'But if you engaged elsewhere, he could go for you.'

'How would you like it yourself?' I said. 'Indeed, however bad he is, I'll spend a year there anyway.'

'I'm sure you will. Ah well, then, see you don't engage at Pitlochry fair next year until I've seen you there.'

'Indeed I won't.'

After numerous such Byzantine negotiations at hiring fairs, by the age of 40 Neil MacPhee was bilingual. He had to be. In 1901 he was living in Ruchazie to the east of Glasgow. At the beginning of the twentieth century Ruchazie was a discrete rural village. The dormitory suburbs of the city of Glasgow were quickly advancing, but Ruchazie and its neighbours, Hoggansfield and Millerston, were in 1901 still bucolic settlements within the north Lanarkshire parish of Barony. Neil lodged with a Ruchazie farmer and his family and worked as a ploughman. At home and on the farm, he was of course surrounded by English speakers.

Steam ploughing by heavy traction engines had been known in Britain for half a century. But in 1901 (which was also the year of the first recorded use of the word 'tractor'), and for another 50 years, most farmers and almost all small farmers still used horses. In the dale of the Clyde, farmers used Clydesdales. Nobody in Scotland, possibly nobody in Britain, was in 1901 better qualified in the use and care of draught horses than a man from the western machair of the Uists. Breaking open the ground for sowing crops was largely winter work, so it is possible that Neil MacPhee was able to get back from Lanarkshire to South Uist to help with the Hebridean summer chores. But his income was earned in the Forth–Clyde valley, and there at last Neil found a wife.

At the end of January 1912 Neil MacPhee married Ellen McHendry in St Joseph's Roman Catholic Chapel at Sheddens, five miles south of Glasgow city centre. He was 51 years old and she was a tall, pretty 33-year-old spinster and orphan.

Like Neil MacPhee, Ellen McHendry was an economic migrant. She had travelled to Scotland from County Antrim in the north of Ireland. She found a job as a housekeeper on the Castle Farm at Newton Mearns in Renfrewshire, two miles from St Joseph's Chapel. Neil met her while he was working a term at the Castle Farm.

Ellen MacPhee gave her husband four children before, when she was still in middle age, she went back to Ireland to die. During her short married life, during Ellen's ten years as a wife and mother, her new family followed Neil's employment from one hiring fair to the next, through the farming terms of rural Lanarkshire. Mary Ellen was born in 1913 in the parish of Eastwood. When Angus Joseph was born on 16 January 1915, almost exactly three years after their wedding, they were living in the hamlet of Nettlehole on the outskirts of the municipal burgh of Airdrie. The First World War had broken out six months earlier, but at the age of 54 Neil MacPhee was too old for military service.

Two more sisters followed Angus Joseph MacPhee. In 1917 Patricia was born in Palacerigg, just outside the busy old town of Cumbernauld in the rolling countryside five miles north of Nettlehole. And in August 1919, Ellen gave birth to Margaret – Peigi – MacPhee in Turnlaw Farm Cottages just south of Cambuslang. All of those places, all of those farms, were within half a day's walk of each other, and were very little further from Glasgow city centre.

When baby Peigi was born in 1919, Neil MacPhee was 58 years old. Ellen was 18 years younger, but a sick woman. For a number of reasons, Neil nursed the ambition to take his young family to South Uist. Ellen visited the Hebrides just once.

The MacPhee cottage in Balgarva was too small for her whole family, so she lodged with friends elsewhere in Iochdar. She never returned there. In piecemeal fashion, for at first Mary Ellen stayed with her mother, Neil took their four children back to South Uist. They would never see their mother again. Ellen MacPhee, née McHendry, died and was buried in northern Ireland at the age of 43 in 1922.

Neil was then able to return to Iochdar because his brother Francis was by the early 1920s an elderly man, still single and still childless. For several years before the death of their father Angus at a grand if indeterminate old age – he was somewhere between 83 and 93 – in 1898, Francis and his younger sister Anna had been working the croft together. As a girl Anna Bheag had worked as a fish-gutter in several west-coast ports before returning to keep house for her father and brother in Iochdar. She was also unmarried and also childless. Between them the two siblings had kept in Balgarva a typically open and generous household.

One of Anna Bheag's older sisters, who was not unusually also called Ann and due to her seniority was known as Anna Mhor, had married a Uist man named John Bowie and settled on a nearby croft at Carnan.

In 1882 and 1884 John and Ann Bowie had a boy named Archibald and a girl named Mary. In September 1885 Ann died in childbirth of puerperal peritonitis in her Carnan crofthouse, in the presence of her husband John. She was 35 years old. Her baby, who would be christened Angus, survived.

The grieving John Bowie kept Archibald and Mary, his two older children, hiring a local woman to keep house and care for them. The newborn, motherless infant Angus was sent two miles down the coast to Balgarva, to be raised there by his dead mother's younger sister Anna and her older brother Francis.

Angus Bowie became the son that Anna MacPhee never had, and probably also Francis MacPhee's surrogate heir. They raised him into a healthy young man. They saw him through school. He became the first member of their family in Uist to speak English as well as Gaelic. As Francis reached his late sixties and Anna her late fifties, Angus passed his age of majority at home in Balgarva, caring for the croft and the animals and the seasonal round of rural responsibilities.

The houses in Balgarva stood on the very lip of the shore, so close to the high-water mark that occasionally a spring tide would send a ripple of salt water under their doors and across their floors. Low tides revealed a marine estate which stretched for acres before the thatched cottages: a wet desert of white sand, seaweed and rock. Boulders of ancient gneiss nudged from the soil out to the sea across this no-man's-land of tidal strand. Only their summits were visible, like iceberg tips, and the smooth carapace of those immoveable outcrops had for millennia been polished by the water and the sand.

One day young Angus Bowie went down to a boulder on the foreshore of 52 Balgarva and painstakingly etched his initials in the hard surface. It cannot have been a casual task. Outer Hebridean Lewisian gneiss is among the oldest and most resistant surface stones in the world. It would have been as easy to carve on marble. But with a firm instrument and a lot of resolve Angus Bowie left his mark, in the shape of the letters 'A. B.', for a further century or two on the rocks in the sea and the sand by the croft that he knew as home. Each letter was two inches high, each had a carefully tutored full-stop, each was deeply incised where the retreating Atlantic tide would reveal it for hours to the sun and the rain, before the incoming sea claimed and covered it again.

On 3 August 1914, some time after that inscription was made and shortly before Angus Bowie's 29th birthday, Britain declared war on Germany for the first time in the twentieth century. Both Angus and his older brother Archibald immediately joined the 1st Cameron Highlanders. They were sent to the Western Front, where they promptly engaged in the first Battle of Ypres in Belgium. The battle was ultimately successful. The Allies regained Ypres, but at enormous cost to British regular and Territorial Army infantry.

On 22 October 1914 Private Angus Bowie of Iochdar in South Uist died at the first Battle of Ypres. Twenty days later his older brother, Sergeant Archibald Bowie, was also killed in combat. Both men's names would later be carved in stone on the Menin Gate.

The childless Anna MacPhee had lost a son. The childless Francis MacPhee had lost his able young assistant and the heir presumptive to his croft. Without every one of those three premature deaths, of his sister Ann, of her son Angus, and of his own wife Ellen, Neil MacPhee may never have taken his children back to Balgarva. Angus and his three sisters could have grown up as motherless, English-speaking, Lanarkshire farm urchins, drifting in their teens to the hiring fairs and the coal mines of Lanarkshire or the industries and domestic services of the city of Glasgow. They would never have known the machair, the marram grass, the horses and the hills of Uist.

In 1920 Francis MacPhee was well into his seventies (like his father's, Francis's exact age varied from certificate to certificate, but in his case only slightly – Francis was born within a year or two of 1843). Anna was still just 66 (give or take a birthday) and perfectly capable of running the household. But Francis was by then too infirm for croft work. He suffered from palsy, which suggests he may have had a stroke that left him partly paralysed and with involuntary tremors.

Francis died at home in April 1923. The croft at 52 Balgarva in the district of Iochdar was subsequently assigned to his youngest brother. In his 64th year, Neil MacPhee had a piece of land to plough in South Uist.

His children, Mary Ellen, Angus, Patricia and Peigi, experienced in reverse their father's cultural and linguistic challenge of three decades before. They travelled from an English-speaking household in the Anglophone Lowlands to a place where nothing but Gaelic was heard from one dawn to the next – and where many people, including their Aunt Anna, spoke little else. But they were young, between four and ten years old, and they quickly learned. 'When they arrived they had no Gaelic,' Patricia's daughter Eilidh would say. 'Within a year or two they had nothing but Gaelic.'

Neil built and thatched a new cottage for himself and his children, a few yards away from the larger old family home. Even by the standards of early-twentieth-century Uist crofthouses, it was small, so small that his youngest daughter Peigi would refer to it as 'a renovated bird cage'. The three sisters and their brother were frequently left in the care of their Aunt Anna, who was in receipt of a nominal military pension following the death at Ypres of young Angus Bowie. When Neil MacPhee was not working the croft, he often travelled south to raise cash by labouring on Lowland farms.

The children were sustained after the loss of their mother by the kindness of strangers and friends, and by their faith. Like most of the rest of the people of South Uist and Benbecula, the MacPhees were devout Roman Catholics. 'Religion featured prominently in our family,' Eilidh would say, 'and my mother said it was the mainstay in her life when her mother died and left them bereft.'

They had also a whole new world to explore. The place-names, which before long they understood, are instructive. An t-Iochdar in Gaelic means a low-lying stretch of land, and Baile Gharbhaidh means a human settlement on rough ground. Iochdar is at the northern edge of South Uist, and Balgarva is on the northern shore of Iochdar. (Those Gaelic placenames, corrupted, are echoed elsewhere in Scotland. Yoker is an industrial town on the flat northern bank of the River Clyde, and Garve is a village north-west of Inverness.)

In the 1920s there were few more isolated places in Britain, even in the lonely Highlands and Islands of Scotland. The western Highlands were a daunting journey from the towns and cities of the south and east of the country, along slow, winding, precipitous, rutted, narrow roads. The Western Islands were a long way even from the western Highlands. For that reason and others, they had not been well treated by mainstream Scottish scholars and writers. W.C. MacKenzie, a Gaelic-speaking Lewisman who published a first thorough history of the Western Isles in 1903, lamented

> The early historians of Scotland obviously knew very little about the Outer Hebrides, and their information is consequently the reverse of illuminating.
>
> John of Fordun (circa 1380) merely mentions Lewis by name. Uist, he tells us, is thirty miles long, and is an island where 'whales and other sea-monsters' abound. He mentions the castle of 'Benwewyl' (Benbecula), and says that 'Hirth' (St. Kilda) was the best stronghold of all the islands.
>
> He states that the Highlanders and Hebrideans were a savage and untamed nation, rude and independent, given to

rapine, ease-loving, of a docile and warm disposition, comely in person but unsightly in dress, hostile to the English people and language (and, owing to diversity of speech, even to their own nation), and exceeding cruel.

Andrew Wyntoun (1426) merely makes a passing reference to 'the owt ylys in the se'.

John Major (1521) has nothing to say about the Long Island, except that Lewis has a length of thirty leagues. One half of Scotland, he tells us, spoke Irish (Gaelic) in his day, and all these, as well as the Islanders, were reckoned to belong to the 'wild Scots'. He makes a distinction between those of them who followed agricultural and pastoral pursuits, and those who were addicted to the chase and war, whom he criticises severely for their indolence.

War, he asserts, was their normal condition. Their weapons were bows and arrows, broadswords, and a small halbert, with a small dagger in their belts. Their ordinary dress consisted of a plaid and a saffron-dyed shirt; and in war, coats of mail made of iron rings were worn by all save the common people, who wore a linen garment sewed together in patchwork, well daubed with wax or pitch, with an over-garment of deerskin. The musical instrument of the 'wild Scots' was the harp, the strings of which were of brass. Major confirms the statement of Fordun as to their hatred of Lowland Scots and English alike...

The principal islands of the Outer Hebrides are not described by Dean Monro (1549) so fully as could be desired... North and South Uist, the former with two, and the latter with five, parish kirks, receive scant notice. South Uist is called a fertile country, with high hills and forests on the east or south-east, and well-stocked land on the north-west.

Just over 100 years before John of Fordun wrote his description of 'a savage and untamed nation' whose inhabitants hated the mainland Scots and English without distinction, the Western

Isles had been a Viking province, a part of the Kingdom of Norway. The same lingering suspicion of the Hebrides as a foreign and untrustworthy region informed the other chroniclers cited by W.C. MacKenzie. It would continue to inform their successors. Despite MacKenzie's efforts, some of those islands remained more isolated than others from southern Scottish society, language and culture.

In the early twentieth century the only public transport to South Uist was its ferry service, and the ferry to Lochboisdale carried only goods, mail, foot-passengers and livestock. It was infrequent and often took a day or a night to cross an expanse of notoriously stormy water. Lochboisdale pier was closed for repairs for most of 1924 and 1925, cutting off the island almost completely from the mainland. The hiatus caused local irritation and questions in the House of Commons, but little else. The Uists were accustomed to being isolated. In South Uist itself there were hardly any motorised vehicles and just one main road, which had been reluctantly adopted and then half-forgotten by the seat of local government in Inverness, 150 miles away on the other side of Scotland.

Thirty years earlier the 1896 *Gazetteer of Scotland* said that Iochdar, 'measuring about 14 square miles . . . forms practically a separate island . . .'

Little had changed. In the 1920s Iochdar in general and Balgarva in particular were as far from the ferry port, shops, and savings bank of Lochboisdale as it was possible to go and still be in South Uist. Very occasionally, Balgarva itself actually did become an island. The highest of spring tides – the same tides which washed the earth floors of some Balgarva houses – crept in through salt marshes through the lowest croftland, until the whole small township was surrounded for a few hours by a semi-circle of brackish sea.

Cut off by the tide or not, Balgarva was much closer to the island of Benbecula than to most of the rest of South Uist. The MacPhee family croft looked at Benbecula over two miles of white dunes, beaches and rolling sea. Within 40 years bridges and causeways would connect South Uist to Benbecula and Benbecula to North Uist. But in the 1920s the three islands were still separated by broad and perilous tidal strands. A child could look from Balgarva at the shimmering sands of Benbecula, but never be allowed to walk there, not even when the emergence of a certain reef from the sea in front of his house indicated that the tide had fallen far enough to make the strand fordable on foot.

'It was a very sad, black place when they arrived in the early 1920s,' a relative would say. The Great War had taken a heavy toll from the Uists. Before the war some 9,000 people lived in the chain of smaller and larger islands that ran from Berneray through North Uist to Grimsay, Benbecula, Fladda, South Uist and Eriskay. Between 1914 and 1918 they lost 372 men on the battlefields of Loos and Ypres and in the ships of the merchant marine. It was a disproportionate sacrifice. On average, 2.2 per cent of the population of the whole of the United Kingdom was killed in the First World War. But 4.1 per cent of the people of Uist died. That figure represented over 8 per cent of the male population of the islands, and by further extrapolation meant that perhaps one-sixth of the young and early middle-aged men of Uist were lost.

Eleven of the Uist dead had been serving with the Lovat Scouts. It was of equal relevance to the MacPhee family that, as well as Angus and Archibald Bowie, no fewer than 30 of the fallen were from the district of Iochdar. Almost all of the Iochdar boys had, like Angus and Archibald, died as infantrymen on the Western Front. Most of them, unlike Angus and Archibald, lost their lives at the Battle of Loos in the autumn of 1915. 'Their colonel in the Cameron Highlanders,' said Father Michael MacDonald of Bornish in South Uist, 'was the mainland landowner Cameron of Locheil, whom they blamed for the slaughter. After the end of the war, in the 1920s, the same Cameron of Locheil (Domnhall Dubh) was invited to unveil the war memorials at North Uist and Benbecula, but the people of South Uist refused to have him perform the unveiling ceremony at their own memorial on Carishival above Bornish. Instead, they asked a local woman, Bean Thormaid Bhain from Kilaulay in Iochdar, to carry out the task as she had lost two sons in the war.'

There was a further cost, which many at that time and later preferred to ignore. More than one in every hundred members of the British Armed Forces in the First World War, 75,000 men, 'were pensioned for mental and nervous diseases'. As late as 1922, 10,000 of those servicemen were still in asylums or hospitals. The effect was discernible even in the remotest parts of the kingdom, like a slight surge of the tide from a distant tsunami. During the war years of 1914 to 1918 the number of people admitted to the single lunatic asylum in the Highlands and Islands of Scotland jumped by 6 per cent, before falling again in the 1920s.

Not a crofthouse was untouched by injury or death. The loss of so many young men had a debilitating effect beyond their individual tragedies. It meant that almost 400 Uist women were either widowed or were robbed of a prospective husband. It was neither unusual nor coincidental that in the first half of the twentieth century two of Angus MacPhee's three sisters left the islands to marry and settle far away in

England. The Great War stole hundreds of families from the islands. Their population, which was already in long-term decline, fell by 1,000 people in the ten years between 1911 and 1921. The number of children under the age of 14 in North Uist, Benbecula and South Uist dropped by a precipitous 17 per cent, from 1,750 to 1,452, between 1921 and 1931. The men who did not return in 1919 would be forever revered in Uist memory as the islands' greatest generation: the best, the bravest, the biggest, the strongest, the wittiest, the wisest – and the heroic embodiments of a lost future.

For all its bereavements, its epidemics and its emigrations, South Uist always had grace and joy. The MacPhee family returned to an island easily recognisable to an exile from 30, 50 or even 100 years before. The Gaelic language had retreated hardly at all since the nineteenth century. Its associated oral culture – the songs and fabled stories of the Hebrides – was still heard in every village. Its subsistence crofting and fishing lifestyle dominated the self-sufficient local economy. Government grants enabled many people to move out of the old blackhouses, which they had shared with livestock, into better dwellings. But the technological developments of the twentieth century evaded most people in the Uists. On the west coast machair and beside the rocky east-coast inlets they had no electricity, no telephones (there were not even, until 1939, public telephone kiosks anywhere in the islands), often no running water and certainly no motor cars. They had their land, their language and each other.

A young woman from Pennsylvania in the United States stayed in South Uist for six years between 1929 and 1935. Margaret Fay Shaw lived in a remote southern corner of the island, over 20 miles from Iochdar. She found there the kind of life which Angus MacPhee was living in Balgarva. It was a seasonal round of outdoor duties which had been honed over centuries. The ground was furrowed by hand-ploughs or by horses; potatoes were planted and raised and stored; grains sown and harvested; cattle and sheep walked to market; the cottage thatch mended or replaced. Much of the work was done communally. The annual fuel supply, in the form of peat, was cut from the ground at the same time every year. It took, estimated Margaret Fay Shaw, six men two days to cut a year's peat for one home. People worked together at 'the lamb marking, the sheep clipping, when the men used to shear and the women fold the fleeces, and the dipping to control sheep scab, which was required in Uist by law four times a year'.

Margaret Fay Shaw was entranced by the humour and hospitality of the people of South Uist, and captivated by their traditions. She diligently collected their songs and customs, sayings and stories. One day her friends Peigi MacRae and Angus MacCuish gave her a remarkable verse which had been written by a man called Allan MacPhee from Carnan, the township close to Balgarva in the district of Iochdar at the other end of the island. 'O mo dhuthaich,' they sang . . .

> . . . 's tu th'air m'aire,
> Uibhist chumhraidh ur nan gallan . . .
> Tir a' mhurain, tir an eorna,
> Tir 's am pailt a h-uile seorsa . . .

'O my country,' Fay Shaw translated,

> I think of thee,
> Fragrant, fresh Uist of the handsome youths . . .
> Land of marram grass, land of barley,
> Land where everything is plentiful . . .

The Pennsylvanian was also an expert photographer. She took a portrait of an old man, a celebrated stonemason called Iain 'Clachair' Campbell. Campbell was sitting outside his crofthouse that day in the early 1930s, smoking a pipe. To his left a tangle of rough picked heather lay against a wall. To his right were coils of thick, strong rope. In the middle, in his big bare hands a sheaf of the heather was being expertly woven and extraordinarily converted into neat lengths of the rope.

Iain 'Clachair' Campbell was plaiting heather into rope because he lived on the east coast of Uist, where there was a lot of heather but hardly any marram grass. Out on the west coast machair, in places like Balgarva, everything was truly plentiful. In that part of Uist marram grass was abundant. In Balgarva the MacPhees had no need to make rope or thatch solely from heather. In its season they also used marram grass.

Marram grass, bent grass or beach grass elsewhere in the English-speaking world, *muirineach* in Scottish Gaelic, *ammophila* (sand-lover) in Greek, is native to sand dunes all around the sub-Arctic coasts of the North Atlantic Ocean. Its relationship to dunes is symbiotic: it helps to create them by binding blown sand, and then marram grass flourishes in the stabilised dune.

It grows in thick clumps, and in Europe its broad, fibrous, resilient strands can reach a foot in length. Marram grass has always been exploited by the people who lived near its dunes. In Denmark, where it proliferates on the Baltic coast, it was used for fuel and cattle feed as well as thatch. In Ynys Môn, the Isle of Anglesey off north-western Wales, a Celtic domain 300 miles south of Uist, marram grass was turned into brushes and mats as well as thatch. Up and down the east-coast links of Scotland 'the bents' became a generic term for the sea-shore.

All over the country marram grass was once so commonly harvested for thatch that in places the coast disintegrated, villages and farmland were buried under sand, and in 1695 'His Majesty does strictly prohibit and discharge the pulling of bent, broom or juniper off the sand hills for hereafter.'

In the Uists and other Hebridean islands where the King's writ failed to run, marram grass was used for thatch until the second half of the twentieth century – until, in fact, thatched roofs themselves were replaced by corrugated iron or slate. It was used for practical, playful and confessional purposes. It was woven into dolls, and even into Roman Catholic icons – perhaps half in appeasement. In Scottish Celtic legend, when the fairies stole away a Christian child they left in his place a facsimile made from marram grass. An echo of the Gaulish wicker man, this chimera had human faculties, but had no human soul.

The folklore collector Alexander Carmichael described a typical Hebridean household in the late nineteenth century as being one in which 'The houseman is twisting twigs of heather into ropes to hold down thatch, a neighbour crofter is twining quicken roots into cords to tie cows, while another is plaiting bent grass into baskets to hold meal.' He noted a local saying:

> *Ith aran, sniamh muran,*
> *Us bi thu am bliadhn mar bha thu'n uraidh.*
>
> (Eat bread and twist marram grass,
> And thou this year shall be as thou wert last.)

Carmichael discovered a festive cereal cake called 'struan Micheil' to which batter was ceremonially applied as it baked by the fire, and 'in Uist this is generally done with "badan murain", a small bunch of bent-grass'. Ears of corn were baked by hanging them over a slow, smokeless peat fire in nets made of marram grass.

'The people of neighbouring islands,' said Carmichael, 'call Uist "Tir a' mhurain", the land of the bent-grass, and the people "Muranaich", bent-grass people. Even the people on the east side, where there is no bent, apply the name to those on the west, where this grass grows.'

Apart from making baskets and thatching outbuildings and the family home, as a young *Muranach* back in Uist Angus MacPhee would have used marram grass and heather to make rope. It was a skilled process, but straightforward once mastered. Three strands of grass were plaited into a short string. Three of the strings were then plaited into a thin rope. Three of the thin ropes were plaited to make a thicker rope. Perhaps halfway along the length of the uncompleted plait, three new strands were introduced and bound in to increase its length. The process was continued until a rope as thick and as long as its weaver wished had been created. A crofting household could never have enough rope, but hemp or sisal rope bought from a shop cost money. Well-made grass or heather cords were equally strong. They had a short useful lifespan but they were easily renewed, and were free. Crofting women knitted and sewed; the men kept their hands busy at night by mending nets and creels, and plaiting rope. In a later age plaiting rope would not be cost-effective. An hour's paid work would deliver more than enough cash to buy yards of sisal rope. But well into the twentieth century most Hebridean crofters had more hours in the day than cash. They had too little spare time and too little disposable money, but in the balance they had more of the former than the latter. However long it took them, making such essentials rather than buying them made economic sense.

And as these things do, plaiting grass metamorphosed from a financial necessity into part of a culture. Perhaps because it was an individual rather than a communal exercise, grass-weaving would never assemble the rich store of cheerful shanties and stories that became associated with waulking tweed or rowing boats. It was a private, quiet activity. But it was as common, as skilled and as useful a pursuit as any, and it inevitably became linked with another powerful Uist custom that would also die later in the twentieth century: the horse aesthetic of the machair plain.

Like rope and baskets, horses had been a necessity in the islands for centuries. Unlike rope and baskets, horses were also a substantial asset and a source of pride, status and recreation. Horses must have been introduced to the Uists when there were ships big enough to carry them there, which is to say some 2,000 years before Angus MacPhee went to live in Iochdar.

Once stabled offshore they were not easily replaced or put out to mainland stud. So unique breeds evolved in the Scottish islands, most famously the Shetland pony, way out off the north-east coast of Scotland, and the Eriskay pony, a stone's throw from the south coast of Uist. Both breeds are historical mongrels. They were probably introduced in the Bronze Age, and over the centuries certainly interbred with Celtic and Pictish steeds from Ireland and the Scottish mainland, Viking ponies from Scandinavia, and much later Clydesdales and Arabs.

But they remained sufficiently isolated to retain distinct characteristics of temperament and appearance. They were small and muscular with large heads. They were intelligent, patient, hard-working and remarkably friendly to the humans with whom they had washed up on those distant outcrops of gneiss. They were easy animals to love.

Hebridean ponies were useful everywhere in the hilly, roadless islands. But on the wide west-coast beaches and flat machair of the Uists they became more than pack- or draught-horses. The machair, which ran for 40 miles from Sollas in the north of North Uist to Polachar at the southern tip of South Uist, and for two or three miles from west to east inland, was horse country as good as any in Burgundy or Northamptonshire. There, they could be raced.

The earliest travellers to the Hebrides recorded horse races. 'The natives are much addicted to riding,' noted Martin Martin in North Uist in the 1690s, 'the plainness of the country disposing both men and horses to it.'

They observe an anniversary cavalcade on Michaelmas Day, and then all ranks of both sexes appear on horseback.

The place for this rendezvous is a large piece of firm sandy ground on the sea-shore, and there they have horse-racing for small prizes, for which they contend eagerly. There is an ancient custom, by which it is lawful for any of the inhabitants to steal his neighbour's horse the night before the race, and ride him all next day, provided he deliver him safe and sound to the owner after the race.

The manner of running is by a few young men, who use neither saddles nor bridles, except two small ropes made of bent [marram grass] instead of a bridle, nor any sort of spurs, but their bare heels: and when they begin the race, they throw these ropes on their horses' necks, and drive them on vigorously with a piece of long seaware in each hand instead of a whip; and this is dried in the sun several months before for that purpose.

This is a happy opportunity for the vulgar, who have few occasions for meeting, except on Sundays: the men have their sweethearts behind them on horseback, and give and receive mutual presents; the men present the women with knives and purses, the women present the men with a pair of fine garters of divers colours, they give them likewise a quantity of wild carrots.

That image preserved by the Skye man Martin Martin, of young men riding bareback, using loose reins of woven marram grass and whips of seaweed, could have been caught anywhere in the Uists over a period of centuries. Horse culture was there as prevalent as on the Great American Plains. The tone of Martin's last words on leaving South Uist by boat for Eriskay would be echoed by many a European catching first sight of the Cheyenne or the Sioux somewhere west of St Louis:

> As I came from South-Uist, I perceived about sixty horsemen riding along the sands, directing their course for the east sea; and being between me and the sun, they made a great figure on the plain sands. We discovered them to be natives of South-Uist, for they alighted from their horses and went to gather cockles in the sands, which are exceeding plentiful there.

Hebridean horsemanship was justifiably famous. It was not restricted to men and boys. Early in the 1890s a newly arrived schoolteacher was talking to a South Uist parish priest on the pathway to his church door, when

> Along the road came at full gallop a large white horse with a young woman seated sideways on its back. Just as we reached the gate it stopped and she slid easily to the ground almost before it came to a standstill. I noted she had ridden without saddle or bridle.
>
> After a rapid conversation in Gaelic, she put her foot on the bar of the gate, sprang lightly to the back of the horse which immediately started off at full gallop on receiving

a slap from its rider. It transpired that she had come with some important message from the priest of Bornish, the next parish eight miles away. On my speaking of her remarkable riding my companion exclaimed: 'Oh, that's nothing,' as if it were not worthy of comment.

In 1901 Alexander Carmichael reported that the yearly Uist *odaidh*, or horse races, were dead. 'By a curious coincidence,' wrote Carmichael, 'the horse-races of Norway and the principal horse-race of the Western Isles, that of South Uist, ceased in the same year, 1820, and in two succeeding months . . .'

The last great 'oda' occurred in Barra in 1828, in South Uist in 1820, in Benbecula in 1830, in North Uist in 1866, and in Harris in 1818. In the Small Isles the 'oda' continued later, while occasional 'oda' have been held in all these places since the years mentioned.

In Barra the 'oda' was held on 25 September, being the Day of St Barr, the patron saint of the island; in all the other places on 29 September, being the Day of St Michael, the patron saint of horses and of the Isles.

In Barra the sports were held on 'Traigh Bharra', Strand of St Barr; in South Uist, on 'Traigh Mhicheil', Strand of St Michael; in Benbecula, on 'Machair Bhaile-mhanaich', plain of the townland of the monks; in North Uist, on 'Traigh Mhoire', Strand of St Mary; and in Harris, on 'Traigh Chliamain', Strand of St Clement.

All these places are singularly adapted for man-racing, horse-racing, and other sports.

Carmichael was referring to huge annual events held on holy days, which certainly lapsed during the tumultuous Hebridean nineteenth century. There had been for hundreds of years a confessional connection between the equestrian festivals and the islands' residual Roman Catholic faith. A South Uist priest who was born in 1818, Father Alexander Campbell, wrote later in the nineteenth century,

> At a distance of two and a half miles from Bornish lies the foundation of an old church, surrounded as usual by a burial ground.
>
> This Church was dedicated to St Michael the Archangel and Captain of the Heavenly Hosts. St Michael was the patron of the whole of the Long Island. Of old it was observed as a holy day of obligation by the Catholics of this place, but long since this obligation was done away with. Still, in my younger years, it was kept as a day of rest by the voluntary consent of the people.
>
> There was always great preparation made for this festival. The good wife, assisted by her daughters, prepared on the day particular kind of bannocks called 'struan', whatever that word means. This 'struan' consisted of eggs, cream and other good ingredients which rendered it very palatable. It was made of a very large size and one was made for every member of the family. I heard that during the time I was at college that my good mother baked one in my name, though it was impossible for me to taste a morsel of it.
>
> It was customary for the priest in charge of the Mission to celebrate mass on this day in the ruins of the old Church, where almost all the people of South Uist, Catholics and Protestants assembled, from the ford of Benbecula to the sound of Barra.
>
> All took their ponies with them, each lad having a lass behind him. When the mass was over, horse racing commenced. If the tide answered they went to the strand where there was a most beautiful and long stretch of an even plain where they could try to perfection the mettle of their steeds. In case that the tide was not answerable they were never at a loss as there were other plains which answered equally the purpose.

Alexander Carmichael qualified his comments by pointing out that 'occasional "oda" have been held in all these places since the years mentioned'. The old religious festivals may have declined, but horse racing continued in the Uists well into the twentieth century. In 1922 and 1928 Finlay Mackenzie, the hotelier who in 1939 closed the bar at Lochboisdale to allow the Lovat Scouts a sober passage to Kyle of Lochalsh, won bareback horse races at the Askernish Games in South Uist. Donald John MacPherson said that the horse races held at annual camp appealed strongly to young Uist men who joined the Lovat Scouts in the 1930s.

We do not know whether or not Finlay Mackenzie used marram grass reins in 1922 and 1928. We can be sure that the Lovat Scouts did their best to obtain leather bridoon before travelling to summer camp or going to war. But the tradition was still alive when Angus MacPhee was a boy. He and his father made and used horse tack of marram grass, just as a few miles to the north, in Baleshare, the MacVicar family ran a small commercial sideline by making marram grass horses' collars and reins and selling them to their neighbours.

When the Second World War was over, in the 1950s and 1960s tractors began to arrive in the Uists and the horse culture passed quickly into history. In a few short years the custom of plaiting grass into reins, halters and baskets was all but forgotten by people other than Angus MacPhee. He did not forget it. He could not forget it.

Angus and his sisters enjoyed a peaceful childhood in the crofting democracy of Iochdar in the 1920s. They were bundled together in their small thatched cottage by the sea, and bundled out of it onto the machair or the strand whenever the weather allowed. They lived an indoor and outdoor rural life that, a few decades later, the girls would cheerfully apostrophise as 'pretty primitive . . . but everybody was pretty primitive, so you were no different to anybody else that we knew. There was no class system.' And their upbringing left happy memories – 'Och yes, good laughs. Good laughs, yes.'

They attended Iochdar School, a walk of a mile from their Balgarva croft, with the sea on their left and fresh water lochans on their right. As an infant in 1914, Mary Godden was taken home by her mother from Edinburgh to the neighbouring township of Kilaulay in Iochdar. 'I was at school with them,' she said.

> Angus had a very intelligent family. I never saw his mother, but his father was a very clever man. He was full of old folklore, and stories and rhymes. And his sisters – Mary, Patricia and Peigi – they were very clever. I was good pals with Mary.
>
> But I didn't know Angus much. You weren't allowed to go dancing or anywhere until you'd left school. Then when you left school there were dances – pipers and good dancers – in the school. But I don't remember Angus MacPhee at any of the dances. He kept himself to himself, you know.
>
> The only chances I had of talking to him was, there was a wee shop in Balgarva there, which was run by the MacQueens. I used to walk from home in Kilaulay to the shop. I could go either by the road out there or round by the beach. And usually it was round the beach, which took me past Angus's house. Every time I left MacQueens' shop the MacPhees' house was the next house.
>
> So he always used to be standing at the corner of the house, you know. And I always used to stop and talk to him. But he was rather a quiet person himself, you know, and I wasn't that talkative either! Just a quiet normal sort of boy –

I never ever thought of him as anything other than that. He was a very nice, quietly spoken boy.

His sister Peigi said that Angus was a studious as well as a reserved child. When at nights the girls sat knitting or sewing, their brother would be curled up by the peat fire in their small crofthouse reading a schoolbook.

His niece Eilidh was told that Angus was a great lover of horses ... 'Angus and his pals would be down at the end of the croft, out of sight of the house, riding the young foals all summer long. They would break them in. When the time came for the foals to leave, they'd be broken. His father, Neil, would say, "How did these horses get so mild?"'

Angus MacPhee left Iochdar School in 1929, at the age of 14. His father was still fit and strong, but was almost 70 years old. Angus worked the croft with a view to inheriting it, while also bringing some cash into the house by freelance hire as a labourer. They planted barley and potatoes. They kept a domestic milking cow, and sheep and cattle for market. On Sunday they walked to mass at the old church of St Michael in Ardkenneth. Like his Uncle Francis, Angus MacPhee anticipated an unremarkable life. It could only properly be sustained if it was unremarkable.

In September 1936 Anna Bheag, Neil's older sister and the children's Aunt Anna, died at home. She was 82 years old. Her death was uncertified by a doctor and its cause was recorded as 'supposed old age and natural causes'. The girls were grateful to Anna Bheag, but knew that they had missed their mother Ellen, in small ways and large: 'The bobs my father used to give us, because my mother was dead,' said Peigi. 'My father used to give us the haircut. We had bad luck in our family; about three generations lost their mothers.'

The children began to spread their wings. In 1933, when she was 14 years old, Peigi MacPhee left Iochdar for the southerly island of Barra, where she assisted an English doctor. On 20 January 1934 – four days after his 19th birthday – Angus MacPhee of Iochdar joined the Lovat Scouts Territorial Army unit at Carnan Drill Hall in South Uist.

In February 1934, a month after joining up, Angus passed his physical examination. A medical officer and a recruiting officer both confirmed that at the age of 19 years Angus MacPhee was a perfect specimen of young Celtic manhood. He stood exactly six feet tall. He had a fresh complexion, dark hair and dark blue eyes. He weighed 11 stone 3 pounds, and when he breathed in deeply his chest expanded almost to 38 inches in circumference. He carried no indications of congenital peculiarities or previous disease. He was certified fit for service in the Corps of Scouts.

Angus went to every annual camp. He went off to the mainland for 15 days in 1934, 1935 and 1936, and for 18 days during each of the next three summers. In January 1938 his initial four-year commission expired. Trooper Angus MacPhee was re-engaged in the Lovat Scouts for a further two years. Then he went to the 1938 summer camp.

On a clear morning in Balgarva, Angus MacPhee could see to his south-east the sun rise over the heights of Hecla, Ben Corodal and Beinn Mhòr. He could look north to the 1,000-foot-high shark's fin of Eaval in North Uist. In the middle distance there rose and fell the modest brown hump of Rueval in Benbecula. He lived on a small piece of land. Each side of it could easily be seen from the middle, and even the far south was often visible from the north. But it was central to an infinity of sky and an inter-continental ocean. It was the fulcrum of a universe of shifting air and water which gave it light and colour and life and constant change. It was intensely familiar. Every meadow, every spring, every hillock, every change of atmosphere and tide had a name.

In the foreground, to his right the low green spit that formed the tidal islet of Gualann reached towards the white southern shore of Benbecula. Between the south of Benbecula and the north of Gualann, as he knew but could not see, the ocean raced through a narrow channel. Everywhere was turf, and dune, and white sand, restless sea and Atlantic sky. Before the house at 52 Balgarva was the strand, and that rocky shore strewn with tangle.

One day when the tide had ebbed he went down to the rocks and carved three letters on the adamantine surface of a boulder of Lewisian gneiss. He chose an outcrop a few yards west of the stone which still carried Angus Bowie's initials. Angus MacPhee's Gaelic mind knew the importance of the prefix 'Mac' – 'son of' – to his name, so the three initials he chose to leave were 'A M P'. He etched them beautifully, in the form and shape of a Latin inscription, with a delicate serif at the base of each downstroke. He depressed the crossbar of the 'A' into a stylish, shallow v-shape, like a medieval Masonic symbol or the upper-case 'A' in the twenty-first-century Nylon Regular typeface. When he had finished, he had not finished. He bordered the three letters in a rectangular frame with rounded corners. Then he engraved another rounded rectangle outside the first one, framing his initials with neat and regular and perfectly parallel tramlines in the stone.

Then the Second World War was declared and Angus MacPhee rode up the machair to Lochboisdale, southwards into the storm.

3

THE ROCKY HILL OF THE BIRD

~ 'A significant and consistent change in the overall quality of some aspects of personal behaviour, manifest as loss of interest, aimlessness, idleness, a self-absorbed attitude, and social withdrawal.' ~

On 27 December 1940 Angus MacPhee disembarked at Leith on the south-east coast of Scotland. He was taken under escort by train to Stirling, the fortress at the gateway to the Highlands.

The military hospital at Stirling had been established 141 years earlier in a seventeenth-century townhouse below the castle walls. Its amenities and function had hardly changed since 1799.

He spent three months there in January, February and March 1941. On 24 January 1941 he was put on the 'Y' list, which meant that there was at first some hope for his recovery and subsequent transfer to another unit. But on 4 March 1941 he was removed from the 'Y' list.

The following month, on 5 April 1941, Trooper Angus MacPhee was discharged from the British Army at Stirling

Military Hospital as 'permanently unfit for any form of military service'. Eight years afterwards, in 1949, he was awarded the 1939–1945 War Medal with Star. It was posted on 19 December, in time for his eighth Christmas since returning from the Faroes.

His disability was registered as 'simple schizophrenia'. The World Health Organisation would later describe this as

> An uncommon disorder in which there is an insidious but progressive development of oddities of conduct, inability to meet the demands of society, and decline in total performance.
>
> Delusions and hallucinations are not evident, and the disorder is less obviously psychotic than the hebephrenic, paranoid, and catatonic subtypes of schizophrenia. The characteristic 'negative' features of residual schizophrenia (e.g. blunting of affect, loss of volition) develop without being preceded by any overt psychotic symptoms. With increasing social impoverishment, vagrancy may ensue and the individual may then become self-absorbed, idle, and aimless ...
>
> Simple schizophrenia is a difficult diagnosis to make with any confidence because it depends on establishing the slowly progressive development of the characteristic 'negative' symptoms of residual schizophrenia without any history of hallucinations, delusions, or other manifestations of an earlier psychotic episode, and with significant changes in personal behaviour, manifest as a marked loss of interest, idleness, and social withdrawal.

Patricia MacPhee travelled to Stirling and took her brother home to South Uist. 'His father wanted him back,' said Patricia's daughter Eilidh. 'Everyone wanted Angus back. They thought he could work the croft, that he would take over the croft.'

'He couldn't cope with it, for some unknown reason,' said his youngest sister Peigi in 2004. Peigi was 21 at the time of Angus's return.

My father had him home from the military hospital thinking that he would be alright, that everything would sort itself out. But it didn't . . .

We didn't understand it. We knew nothing about it. We knew nothing about illnesses of that kind, we weren't acquainted with illnesses of that type. Who was? Who was? Nobody here, nobody in this village. And in the village let me tell you, you found they weren't your best friends. They were frightened of Angus. Well he was so tall, and he was so big, and he was different to everybody else, you know . . . Because they were all just ordinary, like we're all ordinary. And he was different, you know.

I wouldn't say he was aggressive. I was thinking back, there was nothing . . . he never did any harm to himself or . . . I don't know how to put it . . . He didn't look after himself. He just didn't look after himself. That was the bit that he didn't . . . He seemed unable to cope. Couldn't cope.

'Nobody seems to know what happened to him in the Faroes,' said Angus MacPhee's nephew Iain Campbell.

He just had some mental problem. He was perfectly ok when he went. So my mother Patricia brought him back from hospital to Iochdar. He must have been here a couple of years, because he was working the croft, but he just couldn't manage. He couldn't look after himself or the animals. I think most of the animals died while he was ill. His father would have been there, but he was quite old by this time. I think his horse died, actually.

And then he would do eccentric things, like pull the cart himself. He would take the cart up to the moor where we get the peats, out at the other end of the township. He'd pull it back with the peats, and seem to have trouble getting it up the hill beside the school. The children would come out of school and hang onto the cart while he was pushing it . . .

'Oh, we had the doctor in to see him and assess him,' said Peigi. Late in 1946 the local doctor suggested sending Angus for treatment at Inverness District Asylum. His report to the asylum said that Angus MacPhee was 'reported to have displayed odd behaviour for some six months prior to admission. He sat up all night, was elated and excited, and went round on all fours at times, barking like a dog'.

'They all thought that he would benefit by it [admission to the asylum], you know,' said Peigi, 'it would be a benefit for him. He just didn't tell you what he felt. He was not a communicator, you know, he wouldn't tell you what he felt.

'They took him in a car and put him on the boat and from the boat they put him on the train and from the train they took him to Inverness. It was a three-day journey I suppose, to get him there.

'I didn't see him for years.'

The first patient to be admitted through the newly opened doors of Inverness District Lunatic Asylum in 1864 was a 42-year-old mariner referred to as Donald D. 'His attack of illness,' wrote physician superintendent Martin Whittet 100 years later, 'was stated to have been characterised by violence, destruction of furniture, and very dirty habits. It is said to have been precipitated by pecuniary difficulties and the loss of his vessel . . .

'He had had a previous history of delirium tremens. Before the month was out, it was stated that he was exhibiting none of these attacks of violence. On the contrary, he was found to be smiling, obedient and cheerful, and so far as he could manifest his feelings, grateful at every little service performed on his behalf, day and night, for he slept little. He was continually muttering or incessantly repeating and shouting at the top of his voice the word "pipe".'

A year later the asylum contained 200 people. In 1946, when Angus MacPhee was housed there, he had 840 fellow residents of both sexes.

Highlanders had for centuries treated mental illness with a combination of shock therapy, care in the community, prayer and punishment. There were several Gaelic words for such an affliction, and even more diagnoses and prescriptions. Certain wells, charms, amulets and incantations were invested with healing power. The *caothach* might be treated in the Hebrides by towing a sufferer through the cold sea behind a rowing boat, or by resting his head on an anvil and swinging a blacksmith's hammer towards it in an awful controlled feint ('he must do it so as to strike terror in the patient and this they say always has the desired effect'). In Roman Catholic South Uist, at least one incantation attributed to St Columba was recited to 'wither the madness' along with a number of other ailments, and 'an autumn Saturday moon' was reputed to be seven times more likely than any other to trigger insanity.

They had no other cures and few other diagnoses.

Under Scots law from the fourteenth century onwards, 'fatuous' people were the responsibility of the nearest male relative on their father's side, and 'furious' people were fettered by the Crown. Scots law might not always have reached into the distant islands and glens, but it touched such mainland Highland burghs as Inverness, where as late as the eighteenth century 'violent maniacs' were imprisoned beneath a grill on the pillar of the town's old stone bridge.

In 1843 a coalition of the great and the good in the Highlands established a committee with the aim of 'promoting the erection of a lunatic asylum at Inverness for the Northern Counties'. While Lord Lovat, the MacLeod of MacLeod, the MacKintosh of MacKintosh and their friends were busily raising money, in 1855 a Royal Commission was appointed 'to inquire into the condition of lunatic asylums in Scotland, and the existing state of the law of the country in reference to lunatics and lunatic asylums'.

The commission reported the story of a 68-year-old 'male pauper lunatic' in the Wester Ross village of Achintee, who had been failed by Gaelic charms and incantations.

> He had been insane for forty years. He lived in a turf house, the roof was leaking and the door, about four feet high, opened directly into the place where the patient was confined, and there was no window or any opening for one.
>
> The turf walls were damp and the floor was of earth. There was no furniture of any description except the bed to which the patient was chained. No bedding except a quantity of loose straw was provided. The patient was wrapped in a piece of blanket, old and dirty, and two pieces of old bed-covering. Except for these bits of rags he was naked. He had been chained for thirty years. The chain was two-and-a-half feet in length, and its end was fastened round the patient's ankle. He never left his bed. His knees were now contracted and drawn up on his chest and completely rigid. He was stated to be occasionally 'furious and excited'. He never washed, except twice in the course of the year.

The publicity given by the Royal Commission to such wretched cases caused outrage. Something clearly had to be done. The Inverness Asylum Committee redoubled its efforts. It acquired an exposed and stony plot of land on the upper south side of Dunain Hill, two miles west of Inverness town centre. (Creag Dùn Eun, its Gaelic original, means rocky hill of the bird.) It was both a remote and, in the nineteenth century, tremendously scenic spot. It looked east over the River Ness flowing towards the Caledonian Canal, the silver Moray Firth and the North Sea. Beyond those waterways the high round hills of the central Highlands rolled into the distant south. Below the hills Inverness itself crouched like a toy town beneath a pall of smoke.

On that hilltop the committee built of red whinstone a grand Victorian sprawl of an institution, two to three storeys high, with decorative high turrets and two water towers. Inverness District Lunatic Asylum would contain more than 350 patients before it was considered, in 1879, to be overcrowded. In May 1864 Donald D., the mariner, was admitted. He was followed over a further 136 years by many, many thousands of others.

The word lunacy, with its origin in the phases of the moon, itself suggests that the Victorians were no nearer than their predecessors or their successors to reaching a reliable definition of insanity, let alone a cure. Inverness District Asylum slowly filled up with an assortment of drunks and depressives, unmarried teenage mothers and middle-aged indigents, sociopaths and socially innocuous individuals who considered themselves to be Mary Queen of Scots or a bumblebee. Their commonality was that they could not be reconciled to their homes and societies because they were a danger to themselves, because they were a danger to others, because they were a financial burden, because they were an embarrassment, or, most usually, for some synthesis of those four reasons.

Although there was a reasonable turnover of patients admitted to the asylum, there was also a good number of lifers. Over a third of those admitted were released within two years. But many of them were subsequently re-admitted; as the decades passed admissions continued to outstrip discharges by almost two to one and the number of patients who died on the premises – frequently from old age – steadily increased.

In 1931 it was noted with bafflement that there were twice as many registered 'pauper lunatics' in the Highland counties as in the rest of Scotland. A pauper lunatic being by definition somebody who was both unbalanced and unable to subsidise himself (few wealthy lunatics were referred to Inverness District Asylum), Highland poverty was clearly part of the problem. The subsistence lifestyle common in much of the rural Highlands at that time did not drive an unusually large percentage of the population mad. But it did mean that families often could not afford to support their chronically sick; they could not without great difficulty carry for a lifetime the burden of an unproductive member. In the late nineteenth and early twentieth centuries in some remote islands and parishes in the north-west of Scotland the system of local poor relief occasionally collapsed because there were too many paupers and too few ratepayers.

Doctors, officials and other experts scrabbled around for the rest of the equation. It was suggested that certain wily but sane Hebrideans had themselves certified as pauper lunatics to win a small allowance from the state. It was stated that emigration 'has drained the Highlands and Islands of much good stock, leaving behind weaker and older people who are unable to stand up to the strain of daily life on the sea coast or among the hills'.

Part of the reason for the boom in Highland lunacy lay in the all-embracing, ambiguous definitions of the term. One in every five admissions to Inverness District Asylum would be for intemperance. Those patients were most frequently discharged after a few weeks, once they had sobered up and dried out – and just as frequently re-admitted. Some men and women were registered as pauper lunatics because they had venereal diseases.

In 1902, exactly one-third of the 157 new admissions that year were 'considered hereditary'. Four years later the strange case of two young sisters was thought to illustrate that hereditary principle. In 1906 a girl from the island of Skye was referred to the asylum with 'acute mania'. Her sister went to visit and found the occasion so distressing that before she could return home, she also 'developed an attack of acute mania and had to be admitted'.

There were orphans in there, and old people who could no longer fend for themselves, and young women who had been willed out of their 'hugger-mugger' communities for the shame of having an illegitimate child, who for the rest of their lives had nowhere else to go.

In 1927 the asylum physician decided that of his 99 patients previously diagnosed as suffering from melancholia or mania, 22 were actually afflicted by dementia praecox. Dementia praecox, premature dementia, or precocious madness, was a disorder characterised by rapid cognitive disintegration, which was usually first observed in the patient's early adulthood. Dementia praecox would itself within a few years be absorbed in the medical lexicography by another delusionary, dysfunctional condition widely popularised as schizophrenia. But when dementia praecox were the words in use, Dr J.C. MacKenzie of the Inverness District Asylum noted that, by early-twentieth-century Highland standards, its sufferers 'tend to lead protected lives, and live long'.

Despite and possibly because of all that, a sense of shame attached itself to the big house on Dunain Hill. 'The dread of the Asylum and the feeling of prejudice against it,' wrote medical superintendent Dr John Keay in 1897, 'once so strong, is happily dying out.' Dr Keay was too optimistic. Sixty-seven years later, in 1964, one of his successors reported that 'a letter arrived from a doctor seeking admission for a patient, saying that she was now willing to come into [the asylum]. Her previous reluctance to do so was because of the stigma attached to such a move.'

That mark of disgrace was not unique to Inverness among British asylums. But it was stronger in self-consciously moral societies, and more pervasive in tightly knit, interconnected communities such as those scattered across the Highlands and Islands. It sprang from pride and dread of public failure. It was of course self-defeating, in that if residency in Inverness District Asylum was considered to bestow the mark of Cain, there was little point in a patient bothering to recover. He or she would only carry the mark back home with them, and once there be somehow tainted for life. For many, their only course after entering the asylum lay either in leaving the Highlands and Islands altogether (which was even in the twentieth century too big a step for a lot of Scottish Gaels to contemplate), or spending the rest of their lives being fed and protected in the increasingly familiar surroundings on Dunain Hill.

In that sense of humiliation may lie another part of the reason why the Highlands had so high a proportion of registered pauper lunatics, and why Inverness District Asylum had so many lifelong patients and so many deaths in residence.

Once inside, fragile Highlanders could barely imagine leaving again. They had no other future. They became, in a twentieth-century word, institutionalised.

Angus MacPhee entered Inverness District Asylum on 31 December 1946. He was one of 137 new admissions to the asylum of 842 patients that year. It was recorded that among the admissions in the previous year, '44 were cases of melancholia, 17 of Mania, 13 of Schizophrenia, 25 of senile states, 12 of mental deficiency, 7 of acute confusion, 2 of epilepsy and 1 of delirium tremens'.

Angus MacPhee was among the schizophrenics. His 'simple schizophrenia' diagnosed in Stirling may have been one of the less aggressive mental and behavioural disorders. But as his family had discovered, it was serious enough.

'Schizophrenia' would be popularly misinterpreted. It did not suggest an unusual level of dual or multiple personalities. It merely implied the same apparent loss of comprehension, expression and capability that could earlier have been called mania, or dementia praecox, or mental deficiency, or acute confusion, or nervous collapse, or even melancholia.

As the twentieth century progressed, the catch-all term of schizophrenia would encompass a number of varying conditions, such as paranoid schizophrenia, hebephrenic schizophrenia and catatonic schizophrenia. Angus MacPhee's variety of simple schizophrenia was often used, as the World Health Organisation pointed out, as a convenient label for a relatively mild form of the disease. It was a schizophrenic disorder nonetheless, and

> schizophrenic disorders are characterized in general by fundamental and characteristic distortions of thinking and perception, and by inappropriate or blunted affect.

Clear consciousness and intellectual capacity are usually maintained, although certain cognitive deficits may evolve in the course of time. The disturbance involves the most basic functions that give the normal person a feeling of individuality, uniqueness, and self-direction.

The most intimate thoughts, feelings, and acts are often felt to be known to or shared by others, and explanatory delusions may develop, to the effect that natural or supernatural forces are at work to influence the afflicted individual's thoughts and actions in ways that are often bizarre.

The individual may see himself or herself as the pivot of all that happens. Hallucinations, especially auditory, are common and may comment on the individual's behaviour or thoughts. Perception is frequently disturbed in other ways: colours or sounds may seem unduly vivid or altered in quality, and irrelevant features of ordinary things may appear more important than the whole object or situation.

Perplexity is also common early on and frequently leads to a belief that everyday situations possess a special, usually sinister, meaning intended uniquely for the individual. In the characteristic schizophrenic disturbance of thinking, peripheral and irrelevant features of a total concept, which are inhibited in normal directed mental activity, are brought to the fore and utilized in place of those that are relevant and appropriate to the situation.

Thus thinking becomes vague, elliptical, and obscure, and its expression in speech sometimes incomprehensible. Breaks and interpolations in the train of thought are frequent, and thoughts may seem to be withdrawn by some outside agency.

Mood is characteristically shallow, capricious, or incongruous. Ambivalence and disturbance of volition may appear as inertia, negativism, or stupor. Catatonia may be present. The onset may be acute, with seriously disturbed behaviour, or insidious, with a gradual development of odd ideas and conduct . . .

[There are] 'negative' symptoms such as marked apathy, paucity of speech, and blunting or incongruity of emotional responses, usually resulting in social withdrawal and lowering of social performance... [and also] a significant and consistent change in the overall quality of some aspects of personal behaviour, manifest as loss of interest, aimlessness, idleness, a self-absorbed attitude, and social withdrawal.

It was not realised in 1946 that Angus MacPhee's age and fractured life made him most vulnerable to the latent condition. Schizophrenia, which can lie for a lifetime as dormant as some malevolent frozen seed, usually surfaces in young men in their late teens and early twenties, and in young women a few years later. Almost no 10-year-olds or 70-year-olds suffer acute schizophrenia for the first time.

It is often triggered by insecurity and physical dislocation. Young immigrants are exceptionally prone to schizophrenia. So are people within the vulnerable age range who leave their childhood homes for more ordinary purposes. Students can develop schizophrenia during their early terms on an unfamiliar campus. And in the late twentieth century it would be recognised that an unusually high proportion of young men manifest the illness during their first year of military service.

In the years before diagnosis and treatment, schizophrenics played different but readily identifiable roles in Western society. The 'oddities of conduct [and] inability to meet the demands of society', which along with self-absorption, idleness and aimlessness were identified by the World Health Organisation as symptomatic of simple schizophrenia, were displayed by Angus MacPhee.

As the World Health Organisation observed, in the absence of a safety net they are also a formula for vagrancy. The same symptoms are evident in the tramps and down-and-outs of the developed world. At its zenith in the nineteenth and early twentieth centuries, between the decline of rural communities and the introduction of the welfare state, the lifestyle of the British tramp could have been framed for a schizophrenic. Simple schizophrenics certainly helped to define the lifestyle of British tramps. Eccentric, aimless, unwashed, unemployable, simultaneously dependent and ungovernable, and harmless to all but themselves: before the welfare state and the motor car, the life of the gentleman of the road was a natural career choice for a simple schizophrenic.

Many seriously afflicted schizophrenics are and always must have been propelled by metaphysical, religious impulses. The mystics and visionaries common in medieval Europe and in much of the rest of the modern world often were and are schizophrenic. The itinerant, dishevelled, mendicant holy men who cared nothing for their personal appearance or hygiene and who spoke to villagers in voices of unimaginable things, would probably be diagnosed as schizophrenic in the twenty-first century. Modern psychiatrists might look at a latter-day Saint Joan of Arc or Saint Theresa of Avila and observe the symptoms of schizophrenia.

The saints were in good company. Another notable fact about schizophrenia was not properly recognised when Angus MacPhee entered his asylum in the late 1940s. Schizophrenics are unusually creative. 'Almost all schizophrenics paint,' said the art therapist Joyce Laing.

> Depressives just walk away from therapeutic work, don't want to know. But schizophrenics all paint, quite strange things some of them.
> The subconscious seems to be stronger with them.

Medication now means that none of them need to be in hospital, but on the other hand none of them can hold down a job. Jean Dubuffet said that they were unable to do anything but produce their own work, that they were self-taught. My definition now is that they couldn't hold down a job in Tesco's for a day. I'm sticking to that. They just couldn't stack shelves for a day. They'd start stacking and then their imagination would start to fly. They'd think, 'What if you made a tower!' And they'd be away...

Schizophrenics are unusually creative in many meanings of the phrase. They are unusually creative because a higher than average proportion of schizophrenics are gifted, unusually because their work is unusual, and unusually because many of them reach peaks of brilliance that mundane humanity can only describe as genius. Their very condition relieves schizophrenics of many inhibitions and allows them to view and interpret the world from a fresh and startling angle, whatever their inventive field.

In the words of Patrick Cockburn, whose 20-year-old son Henry developed the illness while at art college, 'the genetic inheritance that produces schizophrenia... is related to the genetic combination endowing people with exceptionally original and creative minds'. The painter Vincent Van Gogh was almost certainly schizophrenic. The musician Syd Barrett of Pink Floyd was schizophrenic. The novelist Evelyn Waugh fictionalised his own most vivid episode of schizophrenia in *The Ordeal of Gilbert Pinfold*. The Nobel Prize-winning mathematician John Nash, who was celebrated in the film *A Beautiful Mind*, suffered from schizophrenia for most of his adult life.

So have millions of others. Schizophrenia, whether dormant

or active, is blind to nationality, class, colour or creed. At any given time roughly 1 per cent of the world's population either suffers from or is prone to the condition. There are few early warning signs. Henry Cockburn was as a child and a youth consistently 'able, original, likeable and articulate, but ... he could be spectacularly ill-organised, was forgetful of all rules and regulations, and did only what he wanted to do himself'. That describes a normal rather than a worryingly abnormal teenager, and the teenage years almost invariably precede male schizophrenia.

Despite the official statistics, when Angus MacPhee entered Inverness Asylum there were another 50,000 adult schizophrenics in Scotland and probably 3,000 in the north and western Highlands and Islands. Some were quietly struggling to accommodate a mild or half-awakened version of the disorder; some were diagnosed and treated; some were homeless and drunk in the country lanes and on the city streets; others were fighting lonely battles in ordinary homes against their chaotic lives.

'In this hospital and in many others throughout the country,' said Dr Joanne Sutherland, a psychiatrist at Inverness, 'there was a population in the long-stay wards of people who had a chronic form of schizophrenia. They came into hospital in this disturbed, distressed state which went on sometimes for months. In time the very active phase quietened down, but it took often a very long time, and once that had settled the person was sometimes really very impaired, and sometimes just a shell of what they used to be.'

Angus MacPhee, the man who as a fit and fresh-faced six-foot-tall youth had joined the Lovat Scouts, was confused and was very often scared stiff. Away from all the familiar comforts of home, in the darkest periods of his illness he was almost permanently frightened. He was then frightened of everything and of nothing, of things which were not there and were always there. He could wake up frightened, he could go to bed frightened, and the relatively healthy cannot imagine his dreams. He was afflicted by chronic fear. He was no longer sure who he was.

Other, later, simple schizophrenics have used the friendly computer flickering in the corner of the room to tell a dozen moderated psychiatric internet forums how they felt. In 2009 one sufferer explained: 'It's a rare type of schizophrenia consisting mainly of negative symptoms such as lack of emotions (blunted affect), lack of pleasure (anhedonia), lack of motivation and persistence (avolition), poverty of speech (alogia), trouble concentrating and social withdrawal. With no positive symptoms such as hallucinations and delusions.'

In the candid world of twenty-first-century online psychiatric forums, simple schizophrenics became sensitive to the assertion that they were little more than jumped-up depressives. 'The two main differences between simple schizophrenia and apathetic depression,' said the same victim, 'are that one cannot recover spontaneously from simple schizophrenia, and simple schizophrenics don't care much about their condition – it's called "la belle indifference" ...

'I seem to get this belle indifference more and more, and decreasingly often care about me not feeling anything. Really, I feel like I let everything go – my entire life and the entire world. My emptiness is then even supplanted by an almost trancelike state of carelessness, though it never lasts long ... It feels like falling asleep.'

'There isn't a "fine line" between depression and severe nega-

tive symptoms of schizophrenia,' said another simple schizophrenic, 'when I haven't been consistently or even moderately
depressed for over four years.'

'I have "simple" schizophrenia,' said another,

> i.e. the type without positive symptoms... I've had it for
> over a decade... taken that long for someone to figure out
> what was wrong with me. Now the negative symptoms have
> progressed to the point that I can't take care of myself or
> really do anything.
>
> I'm trying medication but it seems the likelihood of it
> helping is very low, because of no positive symptoms. I partly
> wish I had positive symptoms, just so I could have been
> diagnosed when I was around 13–14 (when my gradual loss
> of mental functioning seemed to start), instead of being 24
> and only just now trying medication.
>
> I'm on quetiapine at the moment, doesn't seem to make
> any difference whatsoever (been on it around a month
> I guess). Tried aripiprazole first, but that wasn't a good
> experience... akathisia mostly, but it also made me really
> indecisive, for some reason.
>
> I suppose exercise would help but I can't get myself to just
> do it. Motivation, desire, they're irrelevant, I just can't get
> myself to do things, blah... I have a very high IQ in certain
> areas, but it's useless because I can't study, can't concentrate.
> I feel like I could do anything I want, if I could just... do
> things.
>
> Really I just wish there was hope, maybe in the idea that
> the medication might be able to help me, I just need to
> be patient... but I feel like it won't. I think it's common
> knowledge that it won't.

The disorientation, social withdrawal and poverty of speech
suffered by Angus MacPhee were considered in the late 1940s
and 1950s to be symptoms rather than primary conditions.

They were therefore treated incidentally. It was believed that a long-term cure for or alleviation of his schizophrenia could be found only by addressing some root cause which, once identified and removed, would take away with it the patient's distress.

In the short term, his doctors had the familiar problem of how to ease Angus MacPhee's burden while they searched in vain for his primary condition.

From the middle of the nineteenth century to the closure of the asylum at the end of the twentieth century, physicians and psychiatrists at Inverness engaged in a search for the least harmful and most effective (the two were not often found in the same drug) 'hypnotics' with which to calm their troubled patients. They wrestled simultaneously with the ethical question of how much their patients should be calmed. 'It is conceived that if quietitude is gained, everything is gained,' wrote Inverness Asylum's superintendent Thomas Aitken as early as 1875, 'yet no greater error nor graver error could be made.' Opiates in the form of laudanum or diacetylmorphine (which was legally marketed in Britain under the tradename 'Heroin' until 1924) were often used to soothe excitable people inside and outside asylums, but their use was disapproved at Inverness by Dr Aitken.

Instead, the superintendent recommended the 'sparing' application of such anti-convulsants and sedatives as potassium bromide and a proto-homeopathic euphoric tincture of the plant hyoscyamus. The nurses, attendants and doctors had another weapon. A large amount of alcohol was consumed in Inverness Asylum. In the accounting year 1866 to 1867 the 233 patients drank 17,265 pints of table beer, 681 bottles of bitter and 1,136 pints of porter. They also took delivery of 350 bottles of fortified wine and 304 bottles of spirits, mostly whisky. Two hundred and sixty-five pounds of pipe tobacco helped it on its way. Even allowing for some use by the staff, that gave each patient 81 pints of beer, a bottle of port and a bottle of whisky a year. It may have helped some of them to sleep at Hogmanay.

In 1884 Dr Aitken welcomed the arrival in Britain of paraldehyde. Paraldehyde, an effective hypnotic/sedative which would be used into the second half of the twentieth century, was safe and non-addictive. It had one notable drawback. A third of any paraldehyde dose is excreted through the lungs, and vaporises in the recipient's breath. That caused – as Thomas Aitken noted at Inverness Asylum – night wards full of men and women who had taken this 'best sleep compeller' to smell intolerably bad.

From the 1930s onwards paraldehyde was augmented by other treatments. Insulin, more popularly a therapy for diabetes, was administered to mental patients because of its incidental qualities of memory-enhancement. Tranquillising psychiatric medications – anti-psychotics or neuroleptics – became more plentiful and more sophisticated. And electroconvulsive therapy became widespread.

All of those were used at Inverness while Angus MacPhee was being treated there for schizophrenia. Electroconvulsive therapy was initially welcomed as a potential cure for the primary condition, rather than just another euphoric or hypnotic alleviation of the symptoms. It was a rocket-age solution: it would zap the root cause. During Angus MacPhee's time, ECT became one of the most controversial treatments in twentieth-century medicine.

Convulsive therapy was not new. In the first half of the sixteenth century the Swiss physician Philippus Aureolus

Theophrastus Bombastus von Hohenheim, who was better known as Paracelsus, induced therapeutic seizures in psychiatric patients with an oral administration of camphor. Late in the eighteenth century 'mania' was treated in the same way in Vienna by Leopold von Auenbrugger. In 1785 William Oliver published an 'Account of the Effects of Camphor in a Case of Insanity' in the *London Medical Journal*.

Camphor was all very well. It certainly induced seizures, because it was a highly toxic chemical. By the same token, camphor was unreliable. Although 'maniacs' who had been made to swallow camphor, and then had convulsions, subsequently displayed interesting signs of mental adjustment, they could also fall physically ill or die. Oral dosages were difficult to regulate. Too little would fail to provoke a worthwhile seizure; too much would poison the patient.

In the 1930s the father of twentieth-century convulsive therapy, Ladislas Meduna, gave controlled intramuscular injections of camphor oil to more than 100 sufferers from dementia praecox or schizophrenia. Meduna's response rates were high. More than half of those who had been ill for less than a decade showed significant signs of recovery. It was decided that convulsions cured schizophrenics. The only remaining question was how to administer the convulsions.

In 1964 Martin Whittet, the physician superintendent at Inverness, claimed that 150 years earlier Dr Kennedy of the Northern Infirmary in the Highlands had treated 'with good effect' two mental patients by electric shocks. If so, Dr Kennedy was a lost prophet. The credit for supplanting camphor with electricity in convulsive therapy went to two Italian neurologists in the 1930s.

In April 1938, having tested electrical convulsions on

animals, Ugo Cerletti and Lucio Bini found their human subject: a registered schizophrenic, a delusional and incoherent vagrant who was helplessly wandering the streets of Rome. Cerletti and Bini hooked him up to the electrodes and gave him eleven shocks. He recovered. He then enthusiastically endorsed his treatment. Most happily, a follow-up examination 12 months later discovered him to be well and in employment.

For almost 40 years after Cerletti and Bini's breakthrough in Italy, electroconvulsive therapy not only replaced camphor and most other chemical agents; it became the golden bullet of schizophrenia. The transformational effects of electric-shock treatment were noted throughout the developed world. ECT equipment was installed from Indianapolis to Inverness. It was certainly a palliative: its effects were immediate. It seemed also, by adjusting neurological impulses, to provide a treatment of the primary condition: a malfunctioning brain. In its earlier applications, electroconvulsive therapy has been likened to kicking a broken television set. It was crude but oddly effective, because like a broken television set a completely broken mind can only improve. Often the appropriate circuits were reconnected.

Not everybody was convinced. A new wave of anti-depressant medicines was developed in the 1950s and 1960s. The instinctive preference of some doctors, psychiatrists and lay people for pharmaceuticals and psychotherapy over electric shocks was confirmed in 1975, when a Hollywood film was released.

No other piece of celluloid fiction can have made so huge an impact on clinical practice as *One Flew Over the Cuckoo's Nest*. It was adapted from a novel of the same name by Ken Kesey, which had been published 13 years earlier. Kesey was a member of the American beat generation who drifted into the hippy era of the 1960s. While working as a night attendant at a California hospital he reached the conclusion that the institution's mentally ill patients were no sicker than he was. They were, he decided, simply social outcasts. As the wider community could not accommodate them, it institutionalised and then suppressed and controlled them with powerful drugs and compulsory electric-shock treatment.

The book and then the film of *One Flew Over the Cuckoo's Nest* projected that opinion to the world. It was comfortably digested. It was in chime with the zeitgeist. Electroconvulsive therapy was easily misrepresented and lampooned. The cartoon image of a mental patient with wild eyes and frazzled, electrocuted hair became internationally familiar. It did not help with public relations that ECT on humans had been pioneered by one of the European Fascist regimes of the 1930s. The number of patients treated with ECT fell dramatically, until the storm blew over and it began to grow again.

But the Cuckoo's Nest Effect would never entirely disappear. A sense that society had violently overreacted to people like Angus MacPhee lingered about electroconvulsive therapy. The sense became a prejudice. It was unscientific and largely unjustifiable forensically. A majority of schizophrenics treated with advanced ECT into the twenty-first century – which rather than kicking the television set, focused on specific parts of the malfunctioning brain – continued to register marked improvements, and to credit their treatment for the easing of their pain. But outside their hospital walls the image of Nurse Ratched and her lobotomised victims in *One Flew Over the Cuckoo's Nest* would not go away. It was just too good not to be true.

After his admission to Inverness District Asylum on Hogmanay 1946, Angus MacPhee was involuntarily given electro-convulsive therapy and two episodes of 'prolonged narcosis', possibly at the same time. Prolonged narcosis, or continuous sleep treatment, or somatic therapeutics, was achieved by injecting patients regularly with barbiturates so that they were unconscious or stupified for an indeterminate length of time. The narcosis could be prolonged from a few days to several weeks.

It was a popular treatment for mental illness in Europe in the first half of the twentieth century, and was often combined with ECT. Sleep treatment was primarily the inspiration of the Swiss psychiatrist Jakob Klaesi. While working at the Psychiatric University Institute at Basel in the early 1920s Klaesi theorised that the symptoms of mental illness could be more intimately connected to the primary condition than had previously been realised.

If the hallmark symptoms of schizophrenia were expressions of an over-active nervous system, then narcotic depression of the nervous system might do more than just subdue the patient and make the nurses' lives easier. It could also alleviate the basic primary condition, at least to the extent that the patient was amenable to other treatments.

'Klaesi injected a total of 26 schizophrenic patients with a barbiturate mixture,' wrote the psychiatric historian Mary de Young, 'to keep them in a state of prolonged narcosis for ten days... Eight of the patients improved well enough to either be discharged or transferred to another, less closely supervised, asylum ward; but three of the patients died. Although Klaesi argued their deaths were due to pre-existing medical conditions and not the therapeutic, the fact remained that in all subsequent uses of the barbiturates to produce prolonged narcosis, the mortality rate hovered between 3 and 5 per cent.'

For those reasons and others, sleep treatment fell out of fashion in the later twentieth century. But between the 1940s and the 1970s it found its most celebrated and controversial champion in the British psychiatrist William Sargant. As head of the department of psychological medicine at St Thomas's teaching hospital in London after 1948, Sargant established a 22-bed 'sleep ward'. He used prolonged narcosis not only for its own supposed benefits, but also to make patients amenable to other treatments such as electroconvulsive therapy.

'Many patients unable to tolerate a long course of ECT,' Sargant wrote in 1972, 'can do so when anxiety is relieved by narcosis . . . What is so valuable is that they generally have no memory about the actual length of the treatment or the numbers of ECT used . . . After 3 or 4 treatments they may ask for ECT to be discontinued because of an increasing dread of further treatments. Combining sleep with ECT avoids this . . .'

'For several years past,' he said, 'we have been treating severe resistant depression with long periods of sleep treatment. We can now keep patients asleep or very drowsy for up to 3 months if necessary. During sleep treatment we also give them ECT and anti-depressant drugs.'

Despite constant monitoring of their sleeping forms, patients died under William Sargant's regime in London. Those mortalities and the transparent abuse of the human rights of people who were given extreme treatments without their consent or against their will led to the discrediting and discontinuation of prolonged narcosis.

But while it was still commonplace, at Inverness in the late 1940s Angus MacPhee was twice sent into a long sleep with injections of barbiturates. On at least one of those occasions – and probably during both of them – he was given electroconvulsive therapy while he was unconscious or semi-conscious.

It did not kill him. It may even have helped to ease his state of mind. In 1950 Angus MacPhee was reported to be 'disorientated – odd habits, washes slippers, little change in condition', but there was no recorded repetition of the 'manic episodes' that had provoked his admission to the asylum. He was soon taken off all medication. The only drugs which he would take in later life were for the physical disabilities that came with old age. In 1993 it was decided that he had suffered in the 1940s from an 'affective disorder and that the initial illness was a manic episode'.

An affective disorder does not preclude schizophrenia, but it is a more refined and less permanent diagnosis. Affective disorders are 'characterized by dramatic changes or extremes of mood. Affective disorders may include manic (elevated, expansive, or irritable mood with hyperactivity, pressured speech, and inflated self-esteem) or depressive (dejected mood with disinterest in life, sleep disturbance, agitation, and feelings of worthlessness or guilt) episodes, and often combinations of the two.'

By 1993 they had probably discovered what afflicted Angus MacPhee. By the 1990s, the specialists also noted, he had become 'institutionalised'.

In the late 1940s he was simply another mystifying soul. Disorientated by ECT, barbiturates and neuroleptic drugs, Angus MacPhee went to work on the hospital farm. There he would evolve a therapy of his own.

4

SELF-MEDICATING

‿ 'They varied from, like Panama hats, to peaked caps, to American baseball-type, sometimes a straw fore-and-aft, sometimes one of the flat-peaked caps that old gentlemen used to wear.' ‿

The hospital had grown and grown. In 1947, the first full year of Angus MacPhee's residence and a year before it was taken over by the new British National Health Service, Inverness District Asylum was renamed Craig Dunain Hospital. It had 852 patients.

In the light of new diagnostics in the post-war years another comparative analysis was made of Highland mental illness. It turned out that if admissions to Craig Dunain were credible, Highlanders' mental health was still twice as bad as the Scottish average. There were in the Highlands and Islands proportionately fewer paranoiacs and fewer manic depressives than in the rest of the country. But there were more neurotics and more hysterics. There were three times as many alcoholics and almost seven times as many melancholics. 'The Highland

Above. 'A wet desert of white sand, seaweed and rock' – looking towards Benbecula from the MacPhees' croft in South Uist

Left. Two Uist crofters in 1960 with a coil of heather rope (Dr Kenneth Robertson)

Below. Leaving his mark on his land: Angus MacPhee's initials, lovingly carved on an outcrop of gneiss before he went to war.

The last of the horse soldiers: Angus leaving Uist on his 'fine gelding' in September 1939

The grand Victorian sprawl of Inverness District Lunatic Asylum, later Craig Dunain Hospital, early in the 20th century

Angus MacPhee: 'He wouldn't talk to anyone in the ward. He would ... start gathering all the different things that, you know, the grasses, and then he would weave them. He did it, and that was that.'

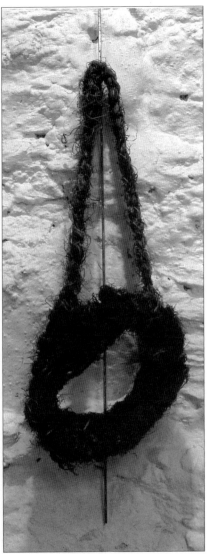

Sowing pouches woven by Angus from grass (Norman MacLeod/ Taigh Chearsabhagh)

Horse's harness (Norman MacLeod/ Taigh Chearsabhagh)

Faded and misshapen by time, Angus's giant grass and wildflower sweater (Norman MacLeod/Taigh Chearsabhagh)

A grass creel or pouch (Norman MacLeod/Taigh Chearsabhagh)

A wader, as worn in its more usual water-proof form by anglers in Highland lochs (Norman MacLeod/Taigh Chearsabhagh)

A rope of grass and beech leaves (Norman MacLeod/Taigh Chearsabhagh)

A pair of grass and flower boots, 'like three-dimensional drafts of a still life by Van Gogh' (Norman MacLeod/Taigh Chearsabhagh)

A pair of 'large but perfectly functional' beech-leaf sandals (Norman MacLeod/Taigh Chearsabhagh)

'Nurses say he sometimes chooses not to reply to people. He looks after his own needs. He is very clean and tidy. He reads newspapers' (Tim Neat/Joyce Laing)

Joyce Laing in the grounds of Craig Dunain, wearing a pony halter made of beech leaves and holding the grass wader (Joyce Laing)

Joyce Laing: 'Once I said, I want a hat, Angus. Make me a hat. And of course he ignored me as he always did. I went away and had lunch and so on, went back and he wasn't there. He'd gone away somewhere in the grounds. But he'd left what he was working on, and there was this Davy Crockett hat …' (Joyce Laing)

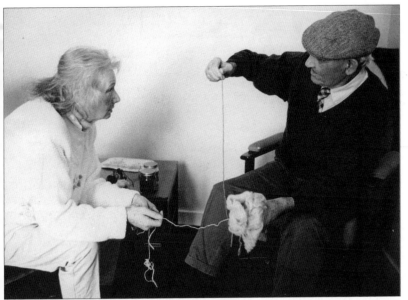

Above. Joyce Laing and Angus MacPhee in Uist House, 1996 (Tim Neat/Joyce Laing)

Left. Other Scottish Outsider Art – one of the enigmatic stone heads of Adam Christie (Norman MacLeod/Taigh Chearsabhagh)

Top. Mrs Flora Johnstone's shell bus in Iochdar, South Uist, as it began to disintegrate in 1990 (Neil King)

Above. Flora Johnstone's raw materials: sea-shells glued into the lids of storage jars (Norman MacLeod/Taigh Chearsabhagh)

Right. Rest and peace, within sight of the marram grass dunes and a few yards from the western ocean

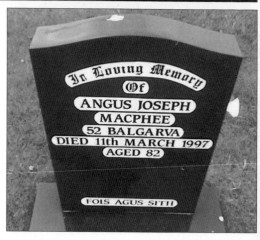

In Loving Memory
Of
ANGUS JOSEPH
MACPHEE
52 BALGARVA
DIED 11th MARCH 1997
AGED 82

FOIS AGUS SITH

temperament,' said Dr Martin Whittet ruefully, 'has a gifted capacity for the gay as well as the grave occasion.'

While the population of the Highlands fell, the population of Craig Dunain grew. In 1901 there were 352,371 people in the crofting counties of the Scottish Highlands and Islands, and 583 people in Inverness District Asylum. In 1961 there were 277,948 people in the Highlands, and 1,051 people in Craig Dunain Hospital. It was not a question of transference – the missing people did not all move into dormitory wards on the south slope of Dunain Hill. But a community and its ancient culture were draining away, which makes them difficult statistics to ignore. While the population of the region fell by 20 per cent, the population of the hospital grew by 80 per cent. At the beginning of the twentieth century 0.16 per cent of the Highland population was registered as mentally ill. By the middle of the century, almost 0.4 per cent was in Craig Dunain. There was either an unusually generous admissions policy at the old Inverness Asylum, or there were causal connections to be made elsewhere.

Only in schizophrenia, that most universal of illnesses, was there some equivalence. In the whole of Scotland in the middle of the twentieth century, 50 people in every 100,000 were annually diagnosed as schizophrenic. At the same time, each year on average 65 out of every 100,000 Highlanders were referred with schizophrenia to Craig Dunain Hospital, in what a contemporary psychiatrist called 'the somatic and medicinal era of Cardiozol, insulin, electro-shock ... and various brands of tranquillisers and antidepressants'.

Craig Dunain had itself expanded sideways to meet the ballooning demand for places. In 1903 the Inverness District Board of Lunacy had bought Kinmylies Farm for the asylum.

It was a substantial acquisition. Kinmylies was a mansion house with outbuildings and 200 acres adjoining the northern boundary of the asylum grounds. The board bought it for £17,000 as a working farm, including 'stock, crop, implements and valuations'.

Twenty-nine years later, in 1932, the hospital's population had risen to 750 and the board paid £4,000 for Milend Farm, another 117 acres of good arable land adjacent to Kinmylies. A neighbouring croft was added in 1944, and by the time that Angus MacPhee arrived there the hospital's farming estate amounted to 400 acres.

Its function was both practical and medical. The farmhouse and other buildings provided extra accommodation for the growing asylum. Many if not most of the hospital's male inmates came from rural communities and were accustomed to agricultural labour. Farm managers were brought in from outside, but at its peak 200 male patients worked on Kinmylies Farm and 'great stress ... was placed at that time on the therapeutic value of the occupation of patients on regular open air employment'.

Their employment was of course unpaid. The superintendent of Inverness District Asylum at the time of the initial purchase in 1903, Dr John Keay, 'said he did not wish to speak of the profit likely to be derived from Kinmylies', but in the middle of the twentieth century the hospital's treasurer wrote that the farm provided Craig Dunain Hospital 'with the bulk of its requirements of milk, eggs, poultry, potatoes and vegetables'.

Angus MacPhee was lodged in the farm ward and put to work with the animals. His knowledge of horses and cattle in particular was quickly noted and utilised. 'He was very, very good, Angus,' said the farm manager Jock MacKay. 'He knew everything about the farm, and he didn't need any supervising. See, they could put him away to a job himself, and he would do it. You know, that was his style.'

He got up in the morning at 7 a.m., ate his breakfast and went out to the fields. He returned for meals. His appetite was always good – 'Angus enjoys his food and eats anything.' He smoked roll-up cigarettes but was never discovered to suffer from a respiratory ailment. He read newspapers. His nurses were occasionally irritated by such of his bachelor habits as stuffing his coat pockets with 'rubbish'. At night he was given a tot of whisky which, it was noted, 'relaxed him'. He did not 'express emotion at all'. He went to bed between 9 p.m. and 10 p.m. He slept well.

After supper, rather than join his fellow patients in their armchairs and doze away the evening, he went outside again. There he did something unusual. 'Very untidy,' said a nurse's report. 'Takes grass and leaves into ward, these he makes into ropes, socks, etc.'

'Patient continues his weaving activities,' said others. 'Keeps himself busy outside weaving grass and leaves.'

'Continues to go about the grounds gathering long grass to make into various things.'

'Out in hospital grounds most of the day. Still makes weird and wonderful objects from grass he collects. Has to be reminded not to bring it into ward.'

'Still making things with straw. Very talented with this.'

'Quite happy working with his grass designs.'

'He spends his time walking round the grounds,' reported a consultant psychiatrist, 'making rope from the long grasses which he pulls. Sometimes he fashions these grass ropes into other items. This is quite a unique "craft" which he is interested in and spends hours at it.'

Angus MacPhee strolled quietly in the gloaming through the farm estate, plucking and weaving grass with his fingers. He would never publicly acknowledge it, but he began to make into an art form the dying traditions of the island which he had lost and found and then lost again.

'What is found quite frequently in schizophrenia,' said Dr Joanne Sutherland, 'is a loss of the sense of self, a loss of the ego boundary. This is very tormenting, and it is real suffering, when people feel this. And sometimes it's evidenced by them doing things that are an attempt to sort of find themselves and find their identity – re-find it, really.'

In weaving grass, Angus MacPhee was doing something that helped him to relocate his identity. He was self-medicating – he had discovered a singular form of therapeutic treatment. He found an activity that calmed him and even made him happy. Whatever his creations became, that is how they were born, and that is how he personally perceived them for the rest of his life.

The fear and insecurity inherent in his condition caused him to turn back with yearning to the last time that he had been content within himself. That was in South Uist in the late 1930s, before the call-up came and before he rode off to Beauly, Nottinghamshire and the Faroe Islands. There were not many features of Uist life that could be recaptured on a hillside near Inverness, but weaving grass was one of them. It also satisfied another demand. Other sufferers attest that restless fidgeting can be an irritating symptom of simple schizophrenia. Weaving kept his hands constantly busy. He very soon discovered that it also engaged, to the exclusion of almost everything else, his mind and his imagination.

'He wouldn't talk to anyone in the ward,' said Jock MacKay.

'He would go in Kinmylies House, get his meal, come out, and start gathering all the different things that, you know, the grasses, and then he would weave them. He did it, and that was that.'

Nothing survives and little is known of what Angus MacPhee wove from grass and leaves and snagged tufts of sheep's wool during his first 30 years at Craig Dunain Hospital. Almost all of it rotted into compost beneath the trees and the holly and rhododendron bushes where he stowed his work in progress and his finished items, or they were raked up and burned by himself and other farmworkers. For the rest of his life he put no artistic or other value on his unique creations. He was not weaving for recognition. What ego, what sense of self he had was too fragile and too precious to be spent on the products of his recreation. He would not and probably could not explain why he was weaving. He was simply compelled to do it, with increasing imagination, ambition and ability as the months and years rolled by. There was, during his lifetime, a label and a premium put by connoisseurs, academics and other artists on his form of creativity, but Angus MacPhee knew nothing of that and would not have been interested if he had known. When in the twenty-first century Henry Cockburn resumed painting and drawing as a therapy for his schizophrenia, his father Patrick noted that none of his 'dark and chaotic graphics' survived, 'because Henry was developing a habit of spontaneously giving his drawings away'.

Angus probably began as he would continue, by weaving from fresh green meadow grass the contents of the wardrobe of a stylish and very large man with many different vocations and interests.

'He made a cap, you know,' said Jock MacKay, 'like a captain on a ship, and he made a coat, a swallow-tailed coat, and he made trousers, and he made boots, and he made gloves.'

Robert Polson was a young assistant gardener at Craig Dunain in the 1970s. 'Angus was an interesting character because he stood out,' he said. 'There were some aspects of mental illness that they still couldn't get to grips with, and Angus was part of that. He was just so distant. He passed you, he wouldn't speak, he wouldn't look at you, it was almost like you weren't there and he wasn't there in a sense either.

'He was a tall, thin, distinguished-looking character. I seem to recollect him in a dark-brown tweed sort of suit, his own clothes. He wore his own hats most of the time, the ones he made of straw. They varied from, like Panama hats, to peaked caps, to American baseball-type, sometimes a straw fore-and-aft, sometimes one of the flat-peaked caps that old gentlemen used to wear . . . I think I saw him wearing his grass boots once or twice. It may have been that he wore them on top of welly boots.'

The hospital groundsman Ian McLellan told the film-maker Nick Higgins in 2004:

Sometimes you would meet him [indoors] in the corridor, but you knew he was on his way out. This was his garden here, his workshop. He spent all the time in here.

And his work was . . . all over here. That wee cherry tree there, there would be bits hanging over the bough of the tree there. But you were so used to seeing bits all over the place. You would speak to him, but you would get no acknowledgement from him, at all, he would just carry on, carry on weaving. The main path here is getting all overgrown now, but he had all his own little routes through these bushes. The feeling of this place . . . you just feel he's still around here.

The 'bits' were lengths of multiple-plaited grass which Angus made, and then hung on bushes or branches or dropped on the ground behind him, as he walked the grounds. Gathered up later, those strips of rope would be the building blocks for his grander items. They would be coiled and interwoven into trousers (with a belt), jackets, waders, boots, pouches and a hundred other biodegradable fantasies.

'Have you seen the way he did it?' asked his nephew Iain Campbell. 'He plaited it, and then wound a bit in to tie all the plaits together. He'd very nimble fingers. It wasn't easy, what he was doing, especially when he was sewing it up. He would make a plait, a big bit, and then he would make a very thin plait, and he would sew it all together with the thinner plait.'

As Jock MacKay and Robert Polson observed, headwear was a speciality. Angus MacPhee made serious hats and funny hats. He made peaked caps and caps with earflaps, top hats, hunting bonnets and the ship's captain's tricorne seen by the farm manager. He made a Davy Crockett hat, and a hat described by nurses who saw it before it rotted or was burned as 'stunning, like a sunburst'.

The sunburst effect was achieved because Angus MacPhee's raw materials were plants in bloom. He wove meadow flowers as red, pink and blue highlights into the emerald green fabric of his jumpers, boots and hats. When the creation survived, its colours faded. After a few months, if they were lucky enough to escape the bonfires, his constructions dried out and turned from soft green grass into brittle brown and yellow straw. It was by definition disposable, auto-destructible art, like a sketch made in the soil before an approaching plough, or an elaborate sandcastle built below the high-water mark.

'And then it all vanished,' said Joyce Laing, the art therapist who discovered Angus MacPhee's work in 1977. 'He'd started it when he came in, he'd been doing it since he came in. I'm sure I missed the best, because when he was younger he'd have been quicker and better at it. Some of the nurses told us, "You know he made like an opera coat with tails?" Of course, we never found anything like that. But I'd have loved to . . .'

Because of the mess it made in the wards, Angus MacPhee was after several years banned from weaving grass indoors at Craig Dunain. But he was allowed to knit inside with more usual fabrics. He gathered clumps of sheep's wool from the fences around the farm. He handspun this unpromising fluff into yarn – a manual process which itself would later be described and become admired as 'fibre art'. He teased out and twisted with his fingers the rough wool until it became threads of yarn. Using two pieces of wire broken from a fence, he then knitted vests and handkerchiefs and scarves and other items, most of which have long been lost and forgotten. Several of the shreds of wool were stained with bright herd markings, and those colours were carefully knitted into the garments.

'So he sat on the edge of his bed at night weaving wool,' said Joyce Laing. 'And he spun, until he got lengths of wool. He got two wires, knitting wires, and he sat with these wires. I thought he'd be knitting, but I've been told by a professional knitter that he was netting, because he'd been taught how to net for the fish. They put them down for these flat fish in Uist which are silly enough to go into nets, so he knew how to make nets. He was making undergarments, vests, and mufflers, squares that looked like hankies – all from sheep's wool. He kept the sheep marking on it – it gave a punch to it, you know.'

He made obvious references to the Uist *muranach* origins of himself and his work. He made horses' harnesses and halters and reins. He made peat creels and sowing seed pouches. Some of them looked like primitive art, some of them looked like three-dimensional drafts of a still life by Van Gogh, almost all of them could under another name be shown at the Tate Modern. They were the echoes of calls from a homeland. Unable to return to *Tir a' mhurain*, he brought as much as he could of *Tir a' mhurain* to a hillside near Inverness.

His silence was selective and illuminating. Never a talkative man, in Craig Dunain Hospital he was almost always dumb. He drifted through the institution like a wraith in search of its former life.

'I never heard him speak,' said Robert Polson. 'Not a word. Ninety-nine per cent of the patients, you could speak to them, like in any other conversation. Sometimes straight away, sometimes it took a bit longer, up to a year, before they started to communicate with us. But Angus would never say a word or speak at all. I never heard his voice. He was almost like a ghost, Angus. He would float past you. He wouldn't look at you. He would just look straight in front of him.'

That reserve was interpreted by many as elective mutism. It would be more accurately described as selective mutism. There was nothing wrong with his vocal cords, but most of the time Angus MacPhee determined not to deploy them, perhaps in silent protest at his removal from South Uist and subsequent confinement, perhaps as another function of his illness or his medication.

Year after year his nurses and consulting psychiatrists made concerted efforts to engage in conversation this man who did not wish to talk to them. 'Angus is a natural Gaelic speaker,' reported one. 'He does not speak voluntarily and only answers questions in monosyllables, although he appears to understand what is said to him.'

'With prompting,' noted another, 'Angus will become involved in short conversations, although he never initiates them.'

'[Angus MacPhee] gives the impression of being contented,' said a typical psychiatric report. 'He was not too keen to talk during his interview. He refused to answer questions about current affairs or the Prime Minister. Nurses say he sometimes chooses not to reply to people. He looks after his own needs. He is very clean and tidy. He reads newspapers.'

When he did speak, it was often to other *Uibhistich*. Those conversations – one-sided conversations, with his visitor doing most of the talking and Angus responding chiefly in monosyllables – were usually conducted in Gaelic. But that was coincidental. It was because relationships between Uist people were almost always conducted in Gaelic, wherever they met, and there was no obvious reason to change that convention. Angus MacPhee was not making a stand on linguistic principle, nor had his mental disorder eliminated the English language from his brain and left only Gaelic. His first language had been English; he was unlikely to have spoken much Gaelic until he moved to South Uist as a schoolboy. Then the overwhelming ubiquity of Gaelic in Iochdar in the 1920s and 1930s quickly made it his preferred, natural, default language. But he remained bilingual.

There was plenty of Gaelic in Craig Dunain Hospital. It could not have been otherwise. When the Inverness District Asylum first opened in 1864, its internal church services were conducted only in English. At that time more than 200,000 of the 350,000 people in the Highlands and Islands were Gaelic speakers, and within two years the visiting minister was 'preaching alternately in English and Gaelic ... There can be no doubt that the change is advantageous, and the conduct of the patients indicates their appreciation of it.'

There were fewer Gaelic speakers in the Highlands when Angus MacPhee entered Craig Dunain 80 years later, and a much higher percentage of Gaels who, like him, also spoke English. But there were still almost 100,000 Scottish people who were fluent in Gaelic, and most of them were everyday users of the language in Highland communities. Unavoidably, during Angus MacPhee's time at Craig Dunain he was in the company of Gaelic-speaking nurses, doctors, psychiatrists, cleaners, cooks and other patients.

But he did not often speak a word to them, in Gaelic or in English. He spoke to *Uibhistich*. He spoke to Jimmy 'Apples' MacDonald, a nurse manager at Craig Dunain who became a Highland councillor. Jimmy MacDonald had moved as a teenager from Baleshare in North Uist to Inverness. As well as building a new life and career, he hoped there to jettison the embarrassing childhood nickname which had been given him in Uist because of his plump red cheeks. All was going well until, walking one day through Craig Dunain, he crossed the path of a patient from North Uist who innocently called out 'Hello, Apples!' It stuck for the rest of his busy time in Inverness and earned the impertinent patient, Jimmy Apples would joke, an especially painful injection.

'I've known him for 30 years,' Jimmy said of Angus MacPhee in 1997, 'since I started to work in Craig Dunain.'

> He would wear a long coat, with a rope that he'd made himself tied around the waist.
>
> If it rained Angus would go into the shelter of trees and collect grass and bring it to a sheltered spot – there was a lot of grass around the hospital to harvest. He made hats, shoes, coats, ropes, horse collars, mufflers, knitted handkerchiefs . . .

People realise now how sad it is that they didn't keep those things and save them for the years to come. I don't think people understood how good he was with his hands and how well he made things, and how apt he was at living out in the woods. If one day there was suddenly no hospital, if Craig Dunain had completely disappeared, Angus would have survived on his own out there.

I'm sure that the publicity he got would have appealed to him. It would have lifted his spirits – knitting grass was his world. That was what kept him alive and gave him the hope to carry on.

When I became a councillor I'd be on the radio. I'd go in and see Angus, and he'd tell me he'd heard me, in Gaelic of course. It was nonsense to say he never spoke to anybody. He didn't say much, but he spoke. Truth is, I'm not sure he should ever have been in there.

While Angus MacPhee was working the home farm at Craig Dunain Hospital and quietly plaiting, weaving and knitting his extraordinary creations, far away the islands of Uist slowly changed. His sisters married. Two of them, Mary Ellen and Peigi, went with their soldier husbands to England. Patricia married a man called Donald John Campbell from two crofts away in Balgarva and stayed at home to raise her family.

Their father, Neil MacPhee, was bedridden for the last years of his life. In 1947, the year after his only son and the natural assignee of his croft was admitted to Inverness Asylum, Neil applied for 'leave to assign his holding at No. 52 Balgarva to his daughter, Mrs Patricia Campbell'. It was an unusual application. Women had hitherto been disregarded in croft assignations. But it was allowed by the Scottish Land Court, and Ellen McHendry's middle daughter became the first registered female crofter in South Uist. Her father Neil died in

Balgarva of natural causes in 1951 at the age of 90 years. Angus could not attend his funeral.

By then a low bridge spanned the South Ford between Iochdar and Creagorry, linking South Uist and Benbecula by road. It was known locally as *Drochaid O'Reagan*, O'Reagan's Bridge, after the parish priest at Benbecula who had campaigned for many years for a safe crossing between his island and South Uist. A causeway across the North Ford between Benbecula and North Uist would be opened in 1960, connecting all three islands for the first time since the last Ice Age and enabling routine social and professional contact between all the *Uibhistich*.

Car ferries began to sail from the mainland to Lochboisdale and motorised transport became ever more common. The ancient horse culture of the island withered away. Foodstuffs such as sliced white bread and bottled milk were increasingly imported, and the days of griddled breads, oatmeal cakes, and a milking cow on every croft slipped into history. Commercial civilian flights disturbed the skies over Iochdar as they arrived and departed from an airstrip built during the Second World War at Balivanich in Benbecula.

A famous American collector of folksongs visited the Uists in 1951 to record on tape what he could of this culture while it survived. 'I have never met a set of people I liked as well anywhere,' Alan Lomax wrote to a friend after returning to mainland Britain, 'and the astonishing number of beautiful tunes that came pouring into the microphone just completely astounded me. If all the rest of the tunes of the world were to be suddenly wiped out by an evil magician, the Hebrides could fill up the gap without half trying.'

A famous American photographer was persuaded by Alan

Lomax to visit the Uists in 1954. Paul Strand recorded the place and its people on black-and-white film. He titled his subsequent collection of island images 'Tir a' Mhurain'. 'In Gaelic, the language of the Hebrides,' explained Basil Davidson in his commentary on Strand's photographs, 'South Uist is known traditionally as Tir a' Mhurain, the Land of Bent Grass, of the marram grass that spreads along its sandy western shore in a myriad of green needles which bend and ripple with the never-ceasing wind.'

A tweed-weaving factory was established in Iochdar in the 1950s. It rose and fell in a few short years, and the men returned to their crofts and their boats. In 1958 a military rocket-testing range was built at Gerinish in the south of the district of Iochdar. In response to the sudden influx of soldiers and their weapons of mass destruction, the local priest Father John Morrison persuaded each village in Iochdar to erect a wayside shrine. Father Morrison also commissioned the sculptor Huw Lorimer to carve 'Our Lady of the Isles', the largest outdoor religious statue in Britain, which was placed on the slopes of a hill overlooking the new rocket range and all the townships of Iochdar.

Electricity arrived in the islands, and telephones and television. New houses were built with roof tiles, and the skills of making marram grass and heather thatch were lost within a few generations. Old Uist was resilient. Its crofting lifestyle and its Gaelic language and culture remained strong in the second half of the twentieth century. But the wholly insular, self-contained pre-war world familiar to Angus MacPhee, the world which had stood almost still for centuries, would never be reclaimed. By the 1960s, few people in Uist plaited marram grass into rope, let alone baskets, and none of them made boots or hats. That tradition was sustained and given the power of flight by a silent, solitary, middle-aged man in the grounds of an Inverness hospital.

But for a happy occurrence, his work too would all have been lost. In 1977, when Angus MacPhee was 62 years old and had been in Craig Dunain Hospital for half of his life, a visitor who would safeguard his unique and strangely brilliant legacy arrived in Inverness.

5

A RARE STATE OF PURITY

∼ *'I was disappointed. We'd heard there was a man made things out of grass, and nobody knows anything about it.'* ∼

Despite being born a few years and even fewer miles apart, Tom McGrath and Angus MacPhee lived in different worlds. Different worlds very occasionally collide.

Tom McGrath, who died in 2009, is categorised as a playwright and jazz pianist. The description is inadequate. McGrath was a prominent mover and shaker in the 1950s, 1960s and 1970s libertarian, metropolitan, beat and hip, art, publishing and music culture.

A Lanarkshire Glaswegian (he was born in 1940 in Rutherglen, 25 years after Angus MacPhee was born ten miles away in Nettlehole), McGrath moved to London in the 1960s. There he performed at the seminal International Poetry Olympics at the Royal Albert Hall and worked on the Campaign for Nuclear Disarmament's publication *Peace News* before helping to found the first British counter-cultural 'underground' magazine, *International Times*.

He returned to Glasgow in the late 1960s, threw off a heroin habit, collaborated with the young musician and comedian Billy Connolly, persuaded Miles Davis, Duke Ellington and the Mahavishnu Orchestra to perform in his home city, and wrote a popular play called *Laurel and Hardy*.

In 1974 McGrath established the Third Eye Centre in Glasgow's Sauchiehall Street. As its original name suggests, the Third Eye Centre was a place for psychedelic and other happenings; a 'shrine to the avant-garde' exhibition and performance arena, it was typical of those which had flowered briefly during the 1960s in London, San Francisco, Birmingham, Amsterdam and New York. It came later to Glasgow, but it lasted longer. Prosaically retitled the Centre for Contemporary Arts, the Third Eye Centre outlived its founder and was still thriving in the second decade of the twenty-first century.

In 1977 McGrath travelled to continental Europe in search of inspiration and exhibits for the Third Eye Centre. In Switzerland he visited the Collection de l'Art Brut in Lausanne and saw for the first time the extraordinary collection of raw, compulsive outsider art which had been assembled by Jean Dubuffet. Tom McGrath's mind, said a friend, was blown.

The Dubuffet collection in Lausanne represented a sea-change in twentieth-century concepts of art. Jean Dubuffet was a French bourgeois artistic rebel. He was born, the son of a wine merchant, in the Atlantic port of Le Havre in 1901. Like other French men and women of his generation, he would live to see two world wars fought on his country's soil. Dubuffet was too young to be enlisted in the first one and too old for the second. It was a recipe for disillusion, disobedience and mutiny.

While trench warfare consumed the east of his country from Dunkirk to Verdun, Jean Dubuffet did well at his Le Havre lycée. After the Armistice was signed in 1918 he travelled to the Académie Julian in Paris to study painting. The Académie Julian was a distinguished and relatively progressive school (unusually, it admitted women, who were doubly unusually permitted to paint and sketch nude models from life), but Dubuffet stuck it out for just six months. He wrote later that a conversation with a teacher had encapsulated his disaffection from establishment art.

The young Dubuffet suggested to his teacher that there must have been, throughout history, forms of art which had been alien to the dominant culture of their time, and which had consequently been neglected and lost. The teacher replied that this was unlikely, because the experts of the past could be trusted to separate the wheat from the chaff. If those hypothetical experts had judged an artwork to be unworthy of preservation, it probably had been unworthy of preservation.

Jean Dubuffet considered such reasoning to be simply stupid. 'Experts' of any age, he thought, were not objective. They were the products of cultural conditioning. In his own time at least, their definitions were moulded by the Graeco-Roman representative tradition, which had become moribund and stifling. His own teacher 'bowed before the prevailing wind emitted by the Establishment, and could consent to find objective beauty only in the place marked out by a superior order'. Dubuffet did not want to be like that, so he left the Académie Julian.

He slipped easily into Bohemian Paris, learning to play the accordion and bagpipes, befriending poets and painting in his own time, in his own way, at his own pace.

In 1925 Jean Dubuffet returned to Le Havre, married, had a daughter, and in 1930 the small young family went back to Paris and opened a franchise of his father's wine business in the capital city.

If the career of a vintner had satisfied Jean Dubuffet, nobody outside South Uist and Craig Dunain Hospital might ever have heard of Angus MacPhee. But at some point in his twenties or early thirties, Jean Dubuffet read a book called *Artistry of the Mentally Ill* by Hans Prinzhorn. It changed his and many other people's lives.

Hans Prinzhorn was not the first European psychiatrist to take a professional interest in the artwork of his patients. Prinzhorn himself inherited the collection of 'psychotic art' amassed at the psychiatric hospital of the University of Heidelberg by Emil Kraepelin. The true original in the field was neither Prinzhorn nor Kraepelin, but was probably a Scot named Dr William A.F. Browne. William Browne was a friend of Charles Darwin and a physician superintendent of lunatic asylums in Montrose and Dumfries between 1834 and 1857, when he was appointed Commissioner for Lunacy in Scotland. Browne introduced such activities for patients as writing, art and drama. He experimented with early forms of occupational and art therapy, and made a collection of the artistic work of his inmates.

But neither William Browne nor Emil Kraepelin wrote the book. Hans Prinzhorn did. *Bildnerei der Geisteskranken*, or *Artistry of the Mentally Ill* was published in 1922. Prinzhorn presented and analysed the work of ten 'schizophrenic masters' from his and Kraepelin's Heidelberg collection. One made obscene figures out of chewed bread until a physician persuaded him to turn to woodcarving, at which he proved unusually adept. Another painted compulsively on his wall with the dyes and juices hand-squeezed from plants. Yet another made designs with animal fat on the wallpaper of his room. 'He always allows himself to be driven by momentary impulses,' Hans Prinzhorn wrote of this man, 'so that his pictures generally incorporate the unconscious components of pictorial creation in a rare state of purity ... he composes completely passively, almost as a spectator ...'

They all had artistic ability, but their subjects, style and motivations were very far from the Beaux-Arts ideal of the Académie Julian and other representatives of nineteenth-century European civilisation. That was enough to enchant Jean Dubuffet. He left his wife and his business and returned to art – but this time, 'There is no art without intoxication. But I mean a mad intoxication! Let reason teeter! Delirium! The highest degree of delirium! Plunged in burning dementia! Art is the most enrapturing orgy within man's reach ... Art must make you laugh a little and make you a little afraid. Anything as long as it doesn't bore.'

While Jean Dubuffet found a new wife and a new vocation in Paris and painted crazed portraits which 'depersonalized most of his subjects, comically exaggerating proportions and idiosyncrasies', across the border in Nazi Germany the psychotic, outsider art collection made at Heidelberg by Kraepelin and Prinzhorn received what in retrospect would be seen as its greatest pre-war accolade.

Adolf Hitler's National Socialist Party, which took power in Germany in 1933, liked 'traditional' art that exalted Aryan purity and militarism. They disliked almost everything else. Most of all, they disliked what had become known as 'modern' art. They called modern art *entartete Kunst*, or degenerate art. It was not only a categorisation; it was a sanction and a threat. German 'modern' artists were, at best, forbidden to sell their work, to teach or even to paint. Some were sent to concentration camps.

In order to illustrate this appalling stuff, the Nazis mounted an exhibition – a counter-exhibition – of degenerate modern art. Five thousand works were seized from private collections and museums by a Third Reich Visual Arts Commission. The 'Entartete Kunst' show opened in Munich in July 1937 and ran for four months, attracting huge crowds, before moving on to 11 other cities in Germany and Austria.

The exhibition contained work by Pablo Picasso, Marc Chagall, Henri Matisse, Paul Klee and Vincent Van Gogh.

It also included, behind the labels 'Madness Becomes Method' and 'Nature as Seen by Sick Minds', some of the art by schizophrenics which had been collected by Emil Kraepelin and Hans Prinzhorn at Heidelberg, and which had been introduced to the world by Prinzhorn 15 years earlier as *Artistry of the Mentally Ill*.

Jean Dubuffet and the rest of the European and American art world and intelligentsia then had several easy questions to answer. Whose madness was preferable, that of Pablo Picasso and Henri Matisse or that of Adolf Hitler and Josef Goebbels? Whose company would any serious artist sooner join? With what authority did the eminences of the Nazi Party disparage others as having 'sick minds'? If the Third Reich proscribed somebody for being 'mad', was it not likely that they were something else altogether, something valuable and praiseworthy, such as challenging, original and subversively creative?

After the defeat of the Third Reich, while Angus MacPhee

was silently settling into Craig Dunain Hospital, Jean Dubuffet travelled to Heidelberg to see what was left of Prinzhorn's collection. He then toured the asylums of Switzerland for three years, assembling his own collection of *l'art des fous*.

Back in Paris, Dubuffet showed his examples of the art of the insane to friends. Five of them were sufficiently enthused to join him in establishing the Compagnie de l'Art Brut – the Society of Rough, or Raw, Art – in 1948. The five were the surrealist writer and poet André Breton, the critic and publisher Jean Paulhan, the art collector and dealer Charles Ratton, the artist and collector H.P. Roche and the expressionist critic and curator Michel Tapié. With the exception of Ratton, whose reputation for dealing with the Nazis during the occupation haunted him for life, it was a company whose eminence grew as the twentieth century progressed.

Dubuffet was perfectly capable of explaining for himself why he thought that art should be discovered outside the academies, the galleries and the museums – as far outside them as possible – and why art produced by people in extraordinary states of mind was valuable. But in 1948, André Breton said it for him. Breton had joined the Compagnie de l'Art Brut, he wrote, because

I am not afraid to put forward the idea – paradoxical only at first sight – that the art of those who are nowadays classified as the mentally ill constitutes a reservoir of moral health.

Indeed it eludes all that tends to falsify its message and which is of the order of external influences, calculations, success or disappointment in the social sphere, etc. Here the mechanisms of artistic creation are freed of all impediment. By way of an overwhelming dialectical reaction, the fact of internment and the renunciation of profits as of all vanities, despite the individual suffering these may entail, emerge here as guarantees of that total authenticity which is lacking in all other quarters and for which we thirst more and more each day.

Those French avant-garde intellectuals were not only arguing that a 'sane' European society which had generated two world wars within 30 years was not to be taken at its own estimation. They were also saying that art created by mental patients, particularly schizophrenics interned in asylums or hospitals, was actually certain to be better than art created by graduates of institutions such as the Académie Julian. Schizophrenic art, psychotic art, *l'art des fous*, raw art, outsider art, or whatever it would be called, was not valuable because it was therapeutic for the patient. It was not interesting because it was a surprise to see it done at all, like Samuel Johnson's dog walking on its hind legs. It was not a freak show. It was the product of a pure human creative impulse, unpolluted by greed for money and recognition and uncompromised by cultural conditioning. It was nothing but art. Raw art.

Jean Dubuffet and his colleagues mounted the first large public exhibition of Art Brut in 1949 at the Galerie Drouin in Paris. Two hundred works by mental patients were shown. In the exhibition catalogue Dubuffet printed his short manifesto, '*L'art brut préféré aux arts culturels*', 'Raw Art Preferred to the Cultural Arts'.

> By this [Raw Art] we mean the works executed by people free from artistic culture, where, contrary to what happens among intellectuals, mimicry has little or no part, so that the creators take everything on its own merits and not according to the clichés of classical art or fashionable art.

> We are witnessing an entirely pure and raw artistic operation, whose creative process is completely reinvented by the artist, using his or her own impulses. It is art which manifests itself. That is its only function. It is not the cultural art of the chameleon and the monkey.

As the London Institute of 'Pataphysics suggested in 2002, it is difficult not to see Jean Dubuffet's post-war career as the inspiration for the Anglo-Saxon philistine scorn of Tony Hancock's 1961 film *The Rebel*. In *The Rebel* Hancock plays a clerk who mistakes his own infantile artistic abilities for accomplished impressionism. His doodles of people and animals are caricatures of Dubuffet's own non-figurative work. The film disregards the fact that Dubuffet and his contemporaries did not create abstract art because they were unable to draw a photographic image of a cow. They could, but did not want to draw a standard cow. They moved into non-figurative work and impressionism precisely because they had explored classical representative art and found it wanting. They had to experience it before they rejected it. *The Rebel* is a sound indication that in 1961 the United Kingdom was rather less ready than France for a challenge to the representative Graeco-Roman tradition, particularly if the challenge was mounted by diagnosed schizophrenics.

Jean Dubuffet continued to collect and to treasure the art of schizophrenics, while attempting in his own work to discover a similar raw purity. He used a variety of different materials in his later 'assemblages', or three-dimensional textural collages. Those materials included such 'found objects' as leaves and grass. Dubuffet lived until 1985. It is possible but unlikely that he heard of the work of Angus MacPhee. It is equally unlikely that Angus MacPhee heard of him. But two sentences by one fit the other like a meadow-grass glove. 'Art does not lie in the beds that have been made for him,' wrote Jean Dubuffet in 1960. 'He runs away as soon as you pronounce his name: he likes it incognito. His best moments are when he forgets his name.'

The Compagnie de l'Art Brut ran out of money in the early 1950s. Jean Dubuffet then resumed personal responsibility for the collection which he had started, and shipped it for safekeeping to the United States of America. It was housed for ten years at the Long Island home of Dubuffet's friend, the Filipino surrealist artist Alfonso Ossorio. In 1962 the collection returned to Paris, where a revitalised Compagnie de l'Art Brut had found a four-storey house on the Rue de Sevres suitable for exhibiting the artworks. Drawings, paintings, carvings and embroideries by mental patients were added, until it contained over a thousand items. In 1967 another major exhibition was presented, this time at the Musée des Arts Décoratifs. Dubuffet published a further manifesto in the catalogue, inviting viewers to 'Make way for barbarism ... The aim of our enterprise is to seek out works that as far as possible escape cultural conditioning and proceed from truly original mental attitudes.'

Although he and his colleagues extended their catchment area to most of France, several of Dubuffet's most important and original raw artists came from his first post-war hunting grounds in Switzerland. Adolf Wölfli, who made complex images often accompanied by a handwritten explanatory text, like a hallucinatory illustrated medieval manuscript, was a schizophrenic from Bern. Heinrich Anton Müller, whose 'The fly-man and the snake' became a classic of the genre, and Jules Dou, who recreated through schizophrenic eyes the legend of William Tell, were both from the Swiss canton of Vaud.

In 1971 the Compagnie de l'Art Brut dissolved for the last time. Dubuffet signed an agreement with the city fathers of Lausanne, the capital of the canton of Vaud, which would enable the whole Art Brut collection to be transported there and put on permanent display in the Château de Beaulieu, a gloriously ornate eighteenth-century townhouse which had once been the home of the exiled French writer Madame Germaine de Staël.

The transfer was completed and the Collection de l'Art Brut opened at the Château de Beaulieu in 1976. Lausanne was immediately proud to declare itself 'the capital of Art Brut (Outsider Art)'.

A year later a 37-year-old Scot, the director of an art centre on Sauchiehall Street in Glasgow, strolled through the doors of the Château de Beaulieu in Lausanne, looked about with mounting excitement, and wondered . . .

Tom McGrath returned from Switzerland to Glasgow in 1977 and walked back into the Third Eye Centre. He saw there a friend called Joyce Laing, who was a psychiatric art therapist. He approached her. 'Look,' said McGrath to Laing, 'I've just come from this Art Brut collection. You work in psychiatry, why don't you have one? If I could get you some money, would you go to the hospitals in Scotland?'

Joyce Laing knew about Jean Dubuffet and Art Brut. She was intrigued. 'I think I could apply for a sabbatical,' she said. 'Yeah, we could do it in a year.'

Shortly afterwards they met again at the Third Eye Centre. 'I've got your money,' said Tom McGrath. 'I've got your money! I've got you money for a week.'

They drank coffee. 'Why don't we do it just for fun,' said Joyce Laing. 'Let's do a circuit of a few of the hospitals and see what we can find in a week.'

∼

Joyce Laing was an alumnus of Aberdeen Art College who, in the early 1960s, became the first psychiatric art therapist in Scotland. In hospitals and sanatoria and clinics on the north-eastern shoulder of Britain, she witnessed the extraordinary creative urges of the human spirit when the body and brain are under duress.

'There were only about 12 of us at art college in the 1950s,' she said, 'and most went off to teacher training, to become art teachers. But I was quite determined that I was not going to teach. I just didn't like the set-up of schools; the clocking in and clocking out. I was one of the few who intended to starve in a garret!

'One of my art friends took tuberculosis and was at the Aberdeen hospital, and he kept on painting while he was in hospital, and he got better quite quickly. The doctors by then knew that there was a scheme going for artists to work with tuberculous patients, and they asked him if he would work with other patients and they'd pay him for part-time work.'

Occupational art therapy for tuberculosis sufferers had been pioneered in Britain by an artist called Adrian Hill. While convalescing from tuberculosis at a sanatorium in Sussex in 1938, Hill passed his time sketching in his hospital bed. He recovered quickly, and attributed at least part of his return to health to the therapeutic effects of his art. His doctors agreed, and invited Hill to teach drawing and painting to other patients.

'My friend did that in the place he was in,' said Joyce Laing,

but he didn't want to extend it when he got home. There were another two hospitals on Deeside and I thought I'd be better working on that kind of thing. I have a medical family background – my mother was a nurse, I have cousins who are doctors. So I applied to the hospital and said, I'm an artist and I know this scheme now, so would they be interested?

I went to meet them, in about 1957. I went to the Glen O'Dee at Banchory, which had been built in 1900 as the first specialist sanatorium in Scotland. There was a matron in those days, and she showed me round this wonderful building, all glass and wood, designed in the Black Forest style, which was the talk of medicine for tuberculosis. Each floor had outdoor terracing that they pushed the beds out on so the patients got the maximum outdoors, the maximum sun.

They were all men because it was run by the government for anybody who took tuberculosis who'd been in the forces – even if they were from Glasgow or Edinburgh they got sent up there because it specialised. So it was basically young guys, the same age as myself, about 70 of them.

I said hello to one or two of the guys and then – talk about interviews – it was, 'Okay, you're in!' It was all under the Red Cross, the Red Cross paid me. I had absolute carte blanche. They didn't know anything about art; I didn't know that much about tuberculosis – so it was, 'Just come in and do what you want to do.'

Those young men were in bed all day, every day, in their twenties! You'd go off your head with boredom. At first they weren't allowed to walk, then they were up for a few hours before being put back to bed. Some weren't even allowed downstairs, depending on their condition. As they convalesced they were allowed down to the dining room, and a games room, and to play croquet on the lawn – it was all an aristocratic type of atmosphere. And they were allowed to go walks in the woods, but not when they were first in. It was very, very rigid, so they were bored out of their minds.

So we got 80 per cent of the population painting. Just because they were so bored. I was amazed by how many patients wanted to paint. I could just give them paper and pencils – all that was supplied to me. They could paint what they wanted to paint.

As I went round they would chat to me about their painting – I want to paint this picture, or I want to paint my girlfriend, or when I was on holiday. So you got this relationship with them. And if they got very ill you got more worried about them. Sometimes they were segregated in single rooms if they were very ill. Some of them said they didn't want to paint, so you just looked in and said, 'Hi, how are you?' They would chat a bit and you'd move on to the next one. It worked in a sense.

There was a boy came in, he was 19, a guy from Glasgow. And the ward sister had said, 'I wish you could get this guy to paint, because he's depressed, and he's very ill, and he's just lying there.'

So I went in once or twice but got very little response, and said, 'Let's just leave it until he's feeling a bit better.' Then I more or less forgot about him.

And it was a priest who was visiting, came running after me one day and said, 'You're the artist?' And I said yes. And he said, 'Will you go in and see John? He wants to see you.' I said sure, of course.

I went in and John said, 'I want to paint.' You could feel the heat from his body, his temperature rocketing up through tuberculosis. He said, 'Not a piece of paper, it's got to be canvas.' I said, right. We had canvases – it was amazing the nurses allowed me to use oil paints, it was all over the sheets and things. But nobody complained.

So he said, 'I want to do a crucifixion.'

I said, 'Do you want to try it out first?'

'No, I want you to help. Tell me what to do.'

I did this figure, this Christ figure. So I left him to fill it in, and I came back a couple of days later – I was there twice a week – and he was very, very ill. The sister said to me, 'This guy is not really able to do anything.'

So I said, 'I'll put it on your wall so you can look at it, and you can tell me next time what you want me to do next.'

The next week I went in, and the nurse said, 'Don't go in there. He died last night.'

That was what you were up against.

But when they were particularly ill, the intensity with which they wanted to produce stuff was unbelievable. That's something I was very surprised by. As they got better, it became just ordinary, amateur stuff.

An antibiotic drug called streptomycin ended Joyce Laing's work with tuberculous patients, because streptomycin became the crucial ingredient in the cocktail of drugs which finally cured tuberculosis. 'A miracle cure,' she said.

You saw the wards begin to go down in numbers, almost overnight.

But in another hospital I went to, all the patients were doctors who had been through the wards and had taken tuberculosis. They were all talking about it when the cure came and beds were emptying, and I was very friendly with men in psychiatry who said, 'That's where medicine's going – psychiatry.'

That was the 1960s, and I went into psychiatry. Somebody must have told the professor of psychiatry in Aberdeen about my interest. There was enough money to build a new 20-bed clinic as a teaching unit. It was called the Ross Clinic, after a man named Ross who donated the money. It dealt in psychiatry and psychotherapy, but concentrated on psychotherapy – you know, the idea of putting psychotherapy before drugs.

The professor heard that I'd been working with tuber-culosis and I'd written a paper called 'Tuberculous Paintings'. He got hold of the paper, and he phoned me one day and said, 'Would you be interested in coming and working with us? We're setting up and opening in a couple of weeks' time. I want a team.'

I was edgy about psychiatry – mad people, you know, and I was in my twenties. But he said, 'Well of course we would train you.' So when I went in, the team was psychologists, psychiatrists, doctors training in psychiatry, nurses training in psychiatric nursing, social workers, all as a team and all working together. Every case that came in was presented and you had to go to every presentation, so you knew the whole history of everybody who came in.

Joyce Laing became art therapist at the Ross Clinic.

I was given a large art studio, absolutely modern, and joiners coming in saying, 'What do you want?'

I didn't realise the facilities were unusually good. I thought, 'This is what you do!' Everything you wanted, you got. Every patient that came in was invited to the studio, as part of their treatment.

It was very high-powered, the Ross Clinic, known throughout the world. Doctors who came from there would get a job anywhere after the high quality of their training. And only a few patients per doctor.

The doctors had never seen the visual side of madness. I would say to the nurses, 'When a patient is brought in, and they're pretty ill' – if they're mad they are sometimes brought in by the police – 'before anything happens, get them to paint. Never mind injections, just get them to paint!'

The doctors would shrug and say, 'They have to be treated too!' But that works, because what we were getting then was their depiction of their visual hallucinations. And some of these patients, after they got that much better, just stopped producing art.

There was one who, when he was admitted – I think they had to get the police to take him in, he was just screaming mad – he painted a lot when the nurses put paints in front of him. When he came over to me he was a lot better, the medication was in, you know. They were given medication and sometimes they got back to normality with it. It didn't last that long, but they'd get over the screaming and shouting and before medication that would have gone on probably forever, on and on and on. But with the medication you get them calming down and they're able to relate, to talk to you normally. And I said to him, 'I got some of your paintings when you first came in, do you remember painting?'

And he said, 'Oh, yeees.'

So we took some out, and they're of a head being distorted and pulled apart – images of hell almost, and beautifully painted, he was very skilled. I said, 'Do you remember doing them?'

And he said, 'I can remember, that was what I saw. That was absolutely what I saw.'

So the pictures were hallucinations. For the first time. Medicine had never seen this before. With the psychiatrists talking and talking to them they were getting a verbal description. But they weren't seeing. And this guy, who was skilled in painting, was actually producing it visually.

It was then, at the Ross Clinic in the 1960s, that I first heard of l'Art Brut. I came across one of Jean Dubuffet's articles. There was a schizophrenic woman called Antonia Jabloner in one of the big hospitals outside Aberdeen, and she had been there for years and years, and she did embroideries – wow! They were just a knock-out! And I thought, this is Dubuffet, this is what he was talking about. But that was all I was seeing. I wasn't seeing any of the others, anywhere else in Scotland.

In the mid-1970s Joyce Laing was seconded from the Ross Clinic to Barlinnie Prison in Glasgow. The largest jail in Scotland, Barlinnie was celebrated for containing the country's most vicious and unrepentant criminals. In 1973 a Special Unit was established at the prison, with the radical brief of rehabilitating some of those offenders through communication and creativity rather than simply punishing them.

It was inevitably a controversial project. After the Barlinnie Special Unit's closure in 1996, Mike Nellis of the school of social work at the University of Strathclyde wrote: 'To some it was a legendary institution, which, through the use of creative arts enabled the rehabilitation of some of Scotland's most violent prisoners, particularly [the convicted gangland murderer] Jimmy Boyle, but which, after his departure in 1980, became a mere shadow of its former self, and a lost opportunity to reform the wider penal system. To others its early years represented a moment when penal authority was inadvertently ceded to critical and manipulative prisoners – Boyle especially – and their unduly liberal champions in the social work and arts communities, which was fortunately retrieved, never allowed to happen again and considered best forgotten.'

Encouraging inmates to involve themselves in the creative arts was central to the work of Barlinnie Special Unit, as it was at the Ross Clinic and at the old Deeside sanatoria. It was no coincidence that following his release the infamous Jimmy Boyle became a sculptor, author and playwright. Joyce Laing was perfectly attuned to the ethos of the Special Unit's promising early years.

And while working there, she took to wandering down for a coffee at the Third Eye Centre in Sauchiehall Street, where one day in 1977 she met Tom McGrath after his return from Switzerland, and where she agreed to embark on a search for Scottish outsider art.

They decided that she needed a photographer on her trek. Tom McGrath introduced Joyce Laing to Jim Waugh, a contemporary of theirs, and another Glaswegian jazz enthusiast who had in the mid-1970s completed a joint honours university degree course in art, history and English literature as a mature student. (Waugh would move into Scottish journalism before becoming best known as Radio Clyde's jazz broadcaster 'Nighthawk'.) Jim Waugh could use a camera. He happily consented to join the expedition. It was decided that 'we'd start at the north of Scotland and work our way south. So Craig Dunain was our first call.'

Early on a November morning in 1977, Joyce Laing drove from her mother's home in the East Neuk of Fife to meet Jim Waugh off the Glasgow train at Perth station. 'But it was a horrible, wet, dreich day,' she said,

and I was fed up with the thought of driving all the way to Inverness, and said, 'We'll get the train, it's so much easier.' So he came off the train and I said, 'We have to get back on the train.'

I say that because when we got off in Inverness we had to get a taxi out to Craig Dunain.

We got into the taxi at Inverness Station, about ten or eleven o'clock in the morning, and I said to the taxi driver, 'Do you know where Craig Dunain is?'

And he said, 'I should, I was a male nurse there for 20-something years.'

So we sat back, fine! Then I thought, this guy was a male nurse, he might know. So I said to him, 'Do you remember anything so strange, so unusual made by a patient that you've never forgotten it?'

And he said 'Oh, lots of them paint and make things.' There was an art therapist there by then.

I said, 'Was there something quite strange, that you haven't forgotten?'

Just as were coming into Craig Dunain he jammed on his brakes. We literally fell forward.

He said, 'There was a man made things out of grass.'

I said, 'Name?' He couldn't remember the name.

I said, 'Ward? I need the ward.' He couldn't remember the ward.

So I said, 'Well I'm going in to see doctors and nurses, they'll know.' And we spent the whole day. There were thousands of pictures – interesting therapeutically, but not l'Art Brut. We'd given up. None of the doctors knew the man who made things out of grass. I thought he must be dead.

I started asking the older staff, 'Do you know what this "things out of grass" is? What is that? It sounds right, for l'Art Brut, what is it? What does he make?' They couldn't remember. So I'd been asking all the older nurses about it. Absolutely nobody had heard of it.

And I thought, well, he's dead and gone and the stuff's gone, and that's it.

And I was just walking with a young nurse down towards the door, and she said, 'Have you had a good day?'

And I said, no, I was disappointed. We'd heard there was a man made things out of grass, and nobody knows anything about it.

She said, 'Do you mean old Angus?'

I said, 'Where is he?'

She said, 'You won't have found him because he's on the farm ward. The doctors don't bother with them because they're all physically fit.'

So we walked down to the farm ward. To my surprise the door was locked. In the 1970s, directors of hospitals had an open door policy. That was the medication of course, you could take your patients without locked doors, they were very proud of that.

But here was a locked door. I rang the bell and this young male nurse came to the door and said, abruptly, 'What do you want?'

We said, 'We've come to see a man called Angus who makes things out of grass.'

And he looked at us and said, 'Don't move. Just stay there. Just stay there. Don't move.' And he shut the door. He didn't lock it, he shut it on us again.

I thought, 'This is a nutty place, I'm going to get out of here . . .'

And then the door's opening again and there's a charge nurse, an older man, and he said, 'What do you want?'

We said, 'We want to meet Angus. He makes things out of grass, we've been told.'

He said, 'Oh yeah, yeah. You'd better come in.' He took us into the duty room. We discovered afterwards the young one thought we'd escaped out of one of the other wards and were a couple of maddies on the run.

So the older man took us into the duty room, and he said, 'Come up to the window. If you want to see what Angus does you'll have to walk down the field, and in the holly and rhododendron down there you'll find his work underneath the bushes.'

It was beginning to get dark, it was about three o'clock, in the winter. But well, you know, we'd come a long way, so off we went down and started to go under bushes.

Jim came out of the bushes first. He said, 'My god, there's a boot!'

Then I came out with another one and said, 'One's left, one's right – it's a pair of grass boots!' With laces and everything – they were just superb. Eventually when I got back to the clinic in Aberdeen I was silly enough to show them off, and the doctors had them on their feet, running up and down. I let them do it, too. Ooooh . . .

I don't even remember what else we pulled out, I was so excited, but we pulled out jackety things, coats, trousers, lots of these pouch things were hung on twigs. They were recent – they were still green.

As far as the charge nurse was concerned we'd got it just in time, because the gardeners burnt it every six months. That was his attitude to it, and of course he was amazed that we were interested in it.

The charge nurse came down and said, 'Is this what you're looking for?'

And we said, 'Yes, this is wonderful, this is l'Art Brut.'

He said, 'You'll want to meet Angus. He's out in the fields.'

Angus's job then was to look after the pony – they were quite good in that way, they'd caught on about the horses, and that he was good with animals. The pony picked up the turnips and cabbages and things. Angus looked after him and led him up and down.

The charge nurse said, 'Of course he never speaks. He absolutely never speaks to anybody. Not to anybody.'

We said, 'When does he do this work?'

He said, 'Oh, as soon as he's had his food he's out doing it.' The others at clinics, they just fall into a chair and half sleep. But not Angus. Angus was always at it. In Dubuffet's description, he was compulsive. So of course we got more and more enthused about the whole thing.

The young male nurse was sent to go and find Angus in the field and bring him in. That was the first time I met Angus. He was wearing a grass hat. He was a six foot tall, handsome-looking man. He had to wear the outdoor clothes for farm work. Just a rough jacket and breeks. But he had the grass hat – like a fisherman's peaked cap. And he was wearing a muffler made from sheep's wool, and a wool handkerchief with the triangle showing from his top jacket pocket. He got that from the fences. The charge nurse was telling us that he pulled the wool from the fences. He said, 'We don't allow him to take the grass into the ward.' You couldn't blame them for that.

They stood there in the fading light, with grass boots, coats and trousers on the ground between them. Joyce Laing told Angus MacPhee that she admired his work and wanted to take some of it away to exhibit in a Glasgow art gallery, and hoped that he would agree. 'He just ignored us – seemingly ignored us, but you knew he was taking in everything.'

She asked the charge nurse if Angus was unhappy with her suggestion. 'If he's not pleased,' said the charge nurse, 'you'll soon know. He's accepting what you're doing or you would soon know.'

Joyce Laing explained that she needed Angus MacPhee's signature on a release form before she could remove anything. The charge nurse shook his head and said that he did not think that Angus could read or write – 'We see to all his needs, so he never has to write or sign for anything.'

Joyce Laing took out the release form and handed it to Angus MacPhee. He looked at it. Then he took her pen, knelt on the ground and rested the sheet of paper on a flat piece of earth. In exactly the right space on the form he wrote, in an educated, copperplate hand, the words 'Angus MacPhee'.

Joyce Laing and Jim Waugh carried away what they could in hospital laundry bags. 'I went back with my car a week or so later and started collecting more,' she said. 'I was silly enough to think, we can't take all of this guy's stuff, even though he did sign for it. It'll be important to him. I hesitated about taking everything. I regret that now. I should have taken everything I got my hands on. But you're still a therapist, you know . . .

'So that was the discovery of Angus.'

Shortly afterwards Joyce Laing wrote a letter to Angus MacPhee at Craig Dunain Hospital, thanking him for his grass and wool creations and telling him of her plans for their exhibition. Angus did not reply. The charge nurse wrote back, saying that from time to time Angus, sitting on the edge of his bed, would take out her letter and read it.

6

THE RELUCTANT EXHIBITOR

*⁓ 'He wouldn't go. I asked him if he would like to
go over to Taigh Chearsabhagh when it was showing.
He just laughed. He thought it was very, very funny
that anybody would want to see his work.' ⁓*

The work of Angus MacPhee was first exhibited in Glasgow in
1978. On the rest of their journey around Scotland Joyce Laing
and Jim Waugh had uncovered several other outsider artists –
or 'artists extraordinary', as Laing was beginning to describe
them.

At Sunnyside Hospital in Montrose – coincidentally the
first posting of the nineteenth-century collector of psychotic
art, Dr William A.F. Browne – she found the stone carvings
of Adam Christie. A Shetland island crofter who was admitted
to the Montrose asylum in 1901, Christie had died there at the
age of 82 in 1950. During his half-century in the institution
he taught himself to chisel stone with a six-inch nail and a
heavy old file. He then turned rocks found in the hospital
grounds into enigmatic human faces and figures, like miniature
Easter Island statues. Adam Christie's work and memory

was preserved after his death by Ken Keddie, the consultant psychiatrist at Sunnyside Hospital.

On the west coast of Scotland they found the vivid, hyper-real watercolour landscapes of the former forester Lachlan Kilmichael, and the 'fantasy underworld of flowers and fauna' created by Mrs McGilp. They uncovered the powerful modernist images of Robert A. All of those artists were prolific and all of their work was visually startling. They were compulsively creative. Mrs McGilp had once been asked to colour some coat hangers for a hospital sale. Having coloured them, she could not stop there. She decorated the bright, newly painted wood with flowers and petals.

Those pieces and others were set beside that of Antonia Jabloner and Angus MacPhee. Antonia Jabloner was the woman whose sketches, paintings and brilliant embroidery in an Aberdeen psychiatric ward had in the 1960s first allowed Joyce Laing to make a connection with Jean Dubuffet and Art Brut. An Austrian by birth, Jabloner was found wandering in the north of Scotland early in the Second World War. She was apparently alone, was diagnosed as schizophrenic, and was taken into psychiatric care in Aberdeen. There, 'she began to produce a vast array of paintings and drawings of landscapes . . . Nurses would allow her to have scraps of old bed sheets and gave her embroidery threads, and without any prior drawing or pattern she would sew some exquisite embroideries.'

Angus MacPhee's grass clothing and accessories – his tunic, his boots, his gargantuan trousers – were hauled, along with their fellow exhibits, up three flights of stairs to the Glasgow Print Studio on the top floor of a Victorian building on Ingram Street. Half a mile away at the Third Eye Centre on Sauchiehall Street, Tom McGrath showed 'Another World', a sample selection of Art Brut imported from the Château de Beaulieu in Lausanne.

'There was a lot of interest at the time in that kind of work, with the two exhibitions,' said Calum MacKenzie, the Print Studio's director. The Glasgow Print Studio had been established six years earlier, in 1972, 'as an artist-led initiative providing facilities and workshop space to artists using fine art printmaking'. The printmakers made a poster for the first full exhibition of Scottish outsider art in Scotland. Beneath the words 'Art Extraordinary' it showed a green tree blooming in a fecund, overgrown garden. Imposed upon the tree was a large red keyhole. The keyhole was a reference to an expression by the Austro-Canadian chemist and art collector Dr Alfred Bader. 'We are only allowed to look through the keyhole into the mysterious garden of these artists,' wrote Dr Bader. 'We can come away. They are forever locked in.'

'I was a bit worried about it being on Ingram Street,' said Joyce Laing. 'It became part of the fashionable Merchant City, but in 1978 it was a pretty rough area. I thought these rough Glaswegians would touch my collection! I was chatting to the psychiatrist in Barlinnie and said, "I'm a bit worried about that stuff on Ingram Street, what'll happen to it." He said, "Have you told Jimmy?" Jimmy Boyle. So I told Jimmy, "I'm worried about my exhibition on Ingram Street, I don't want anybody touching it." "Oh aye," he said. Then I knew it was safe.'

Laing had devised the term 'Art Extraordinary' for her collection because she thought 'outsider art' was both derogatory and inadequate. 'In my own search for this form of art in Scotland,' she would write, 'I soon felt handicapped by the use of the term "outsider".

'Following the repeated utterances of viewers to whom

I showed examples of this art, I began to call it "art extra-ordinary". People would react with gasps of amazement, often they were particularly fascinated by these artists' use of materials, not normally associated with art work. The exclamation "extraordinary!" seemed to belong to the works I had discovered . . .'

Later Joyce Laing would refine her terms.

Art Extraordinary refers to visual art forms created by an artist, usually with no formal art education or training, whose works arise from an inner necessity impelled by intense personal vision.

They paint, sculpt, weave, draw or build because they are obsessively engaged by a need to express this vision in a way which is unique to the individual and hence unconstrained by adherence to any artistic convention. As such, the works do not tend to be created for commercial gain.

Except that they are thus compelled, visionary artists may often be ordinary people from all walks of life, although many are within the care of institutions or have become isolated on the margins of conventional society. Others may be elderly, disabled or have mental health issues.

In several respects, the grass-weaving and wool-knitting of Angus MacPhee fell outside the categories first established by Jean Dubuffet. Angus did not suffer from the worst kind of psychosis. His illness was serious, but he was a simple rather than a paranoid, hebephrenic or catatonic schizophrenic. In his usual condition, 'delusions and hallucinations are not evident, and the disorder is less obviously psychotic than the hebephrenic, paranoid, and catatonic subtypes of schizophrenia'.

Nobody will ever know the moods and mechanisms of

Angus MacPhee's mind, but insofar as it was reflected in his weaving he was relatively untroubled – the qualification 'relatively' is, in discussing schizophrenia, vitally important. He made no images of screaming, haunted men. He did not depict his environment in violent, paranoid colours. He showed no signs of the desperate spiritual yearning that was evidenced in the art of some other seriously troubled schizophrenics. He opened no window – or keyhole – through which psychiatrists might peer into the schizophrenic brain. The work of many schizophrenics might illustrate the contention of Arnulf Rainer that 'madness is the thirteenth muse', but Angus MacPhee had other inspirations.

His imagination was unique and his means of expression was unparalleled. He did not work for money or fame, and he put no artistic or financial value whatsoever on his creations. He laboured far outside the cultural mainstream. In those ways he slotted perfectly into Jean Dubuffet's school of Art Brut.

But Angus MacPhee's weaving of grass had a heritage. That was at least part of its appeal. It did not arrive from nowhere, out of the distant recesses of a troubled mind. It was the last – and possibly the most remarkable – expression of a craft which had been alive since humans first shared the shores of the North Atlantic Ocean with clumps of marram grass, but which would slip within a single lifetime through the careless fingers of the twentieth century. It had an historical and cultural family tree. If Angus MacPhee had stuck to making horses' halters and baskets from grass, he would have remained a traditional craftsman. When, with time on his skilled hands, he turned the craft to making spectacularly useless objects such as swallow-tailed coats, tricorne hats and boots fringed with spring flowers, he raised it to a form of art.

In 1937 Adolf Hitler said of the 'degenerate art' of Paul Klee that it appeared to have been 'produced in some Stone Age ten or twenty thousand years ago'. Joyce Laing said that only in 1991 did she realise the true perspective of Angus MacPhee's work. In that year two German hikers discovered high in the Italian Alps the mummified and frozen body and belongings of a man who had died 5,300 years earlier. His cloak was made of woven grass. His boots were lined with grass inner-socks and had laces made of plaited grass. His flint dagger was kept in a twined grass sheath. On a ledge near his corpse lay a long grass-fibre rope . . .

Whether or not Angus MacPhee understood that he was responsible for the last florescence of an ancient tradition is a valid question to pose. The probability is that in disturbing circumstances he turned to a familiar and comforting exercise. He found solace there. Weaving grass proved to be of immense therapeutic value to him. As his dexterity improved and he mastered the old skill – as much as or more than anybody had ever mastered it – his imagination took flight. He had no reason to make practical working items from grass: the horses on Kinmylies Farm came already equipped with leather halters. So he fed his fantasies, and satisfied his intelligent Uist humour, by making things from grass that no sensible person had ever previously considered making from grass. An innate sense of shape, balance and beauty provided the rest: the fringes and highlights of small wild flowers, the leaves and the changing patterns.

Whether or not Angus MacPhee understood that he was paying homage in its twilight to a millennial talent is irrelevant to any appreciation of his art. He was doing so, and that is enough. It gave his weaving depth as well as mystery and wonder. After hearing traditional unaccompanied polyphonic singing one Christmas Eve in the late 1940s at a chapel in the Corsican mountains, the writer Dorothy Carrington said that it sounded like the music she had waited all her life to hear. 'I had the impression of hearing a voice from the entrails of the earth,' she wrote later. 'Song from the beginning of the world.' The impact is comparable.

Joyce Laing tried to return to Craig Dunain at least once a year after 1977.

His mind must have been, 'Right, I'm making a jacket.' So presumably he started from the hem upward, which you would if you were knitting. The interesting thing about the big famous jacket is it's got a basque, and a big hem in a different stitch. That means he'd worked out that the end's going to have a slightly different stitch to it, and then when it was the main body bit – you get that in a jumper or sweater – he was on to the plain sort of knitting. And then the cuffs, the huge cuffs, had the same different stitch as the basque. But the neck was a polo neck. It was just very thick. I couldn't quite see how he did it. His hands were just going like this, so quickly the whole time.

> I saw him work. He'd make six-foot long ropes before he started to make the garments, he'd have a lot of six-foot long ropes. They weren't perfectly round. He would plait. He had no tools, just fingers. So he knitted on his fingers.

> His mind must have been, 'Right, I'm making a jacket.' So presumably he started from the hem upward, which you would if you were knitting. The interesting thing about the big famous jacket is it's got a basque, and a big hem in a different stitch. That means he'd worked out that the end's going to have a slightly different stitch to it, and then when it was the main body bit – you get that in a jumper or sweater – he was on to the plain sort of knitting. And then the cuffs, the huge cuffs, had the same different stitch as the basque. But the neck was a polo neck. It was just very thick. I couldn't quite see how he did it. His hands were just going like this, so quickly the whole time.

> I would think it took him a day or two to make one article. Probably several days. Once I said, 'I want a hat, Angus. Make me a hat.' And of course he ignored me as he always did.

> I went away and had lunch and so on, went back and he wasn't there. He'd gone away somewhere in the grounds. But he'd left what he was working on, and there was this Davy Crockett hat . . .

He also made a cat at one point, like a child's cat. I think he had a wit, he thought it was funny. The cat had a big long tail and whiskers, it was just a funny cat. And I thought the same about the Davy Crockett hat, that there was a wee bit of wickedness about him.

And the staff at Craig Dunain hardly seemed to notice or care, although art people like me were considered a bit nutty anyway. I would take black bags with me when I went to see him in the '80s. I'd drive my car as near to the ward as possible. And I'd go into the bushes – I knew where he worked – and I would drag things out and put them in a bag. And the staff would stand at the window of a ward and watch me. Never did they say, 'What are you doing?' Never did they come out and say, 'Can we help?'

Angus MacPhee saw the heyday of the Kinmylies Farm adjunct to Craig Dunain Hospital. The asylum's home farm was at its biggest and busiest in the middle of the twentieth century. After that time its function deteriorated. The overall number of patients continued to increase, but fewer of them had agricultural backgrounds. The nationalised Northern Regional Hospital Board began to buy its food and other provisions out of central funding from wholesalers. From the 1960s onward Kinmylies Farm was steadily reduced. Thirty acres of it were turned into an extension to Inverness Municipal Golf Course. A brand new, 229-bed 'mental deficiency hospital' called Craig Phadrig was built on the eastern slopes of the farm and opened in 1969. New housing developments for the rapidly expanding town covered acre after acre of arable and grazing land and steadily engulfed the old agricultural premises.

In the 1980s the farm was run down to closure. Angus MacPhee was moved 'up the top', to the back wards and the gardens of the old asylum.

'He told me there wasna the same grass up there, at the Craig Dunain hospital,' said the farm manager Jock MacKay.

'The farm was closed and he had to move to a ward in the big hospital,' said Joyce Laing. 'That's when he couldn't get the grass. I don't know why he couldn't go back for the grass, but that's when he started using beech leaves . . .'

Angus MacPhee's leaf creations were deliberate experiments in a different medium. Whatever he told Jock MacKay, he could and did still obtain and weave grass, despite its comparatively inferior quality. He began to use leaves as well, because he wanted to.

He chiefly deployed the sea-green, diamond-shaped leaves of the native European beech. Using grass as a foundation material, he constructed a workable pony halter from leaves, a series of small horn-shaped pouches, and a pair of large but perfectly functional beech-leaf sandals, with a flat sole and a single grass foot-strap.

'He took and overlapped the stems of the leaves, leaf by leaf,' said Joyce Laing. 'Of course, they've gone so brittle with time. You can imagine what they were like – the lovely pale lime of beech leaves, but they've gone dull. He made satchels, he made quite a lot of satchels which I suppose people used to take in the peats, or carry tools. When I found them in Craig Dunain, he'd put wild flowers in around the borders. Of course they didn't last – they didn't last as long as grass.'

His delicate beech-leaf constructions were almost purely artistic expressions, if it is possible, as Jean Dubuffet proposed, to create art without an artistic ego. There is no tradition of utilitarian leaf-use in the Western Isles of Scotland. Apart from anything else, there are very few trees of any kind in the Uists. When he wove grass, Angus was drawing on centuries of native craft. When he wove leaves and grass together he was striking out on his own into a form which was recreational and decorative. Angus MacPhee did not see his work in that way, but Angus MacPhee was not like other men. He was neither ashamed nor proud of his creations; he merely disregarded them. That did not make his constructions accidental. Everything he fashioned from leaves or grass was as carefully planned and deliberately executed as the work of a professional sculptor. He just perceived it in a different light. Once it was finished, he had no further interest in what he had made. His focus was then wholly transferred to his next project.

It would therefore have been of little interest to Angus MacPhee to learn that when he made flip-flop sandals or mysterious deep pouches from leaves, he was foreshadowing the work of reputable commercial artists. Andy Goldsworthy grew up in the West Riding of Yorkshire. As a teenager in the 1960s he often worked as a farm labourer. Although Goldsworthy studied fine art at Bradford College of Art and Preston Polytechnic, he would later credit such bucolic experiences as picking potatoes with the inspiration for his 'environmental art'.

Goldsworthy, who moved to live in southern Scotland, specialised in making representative and abstract constructions from natural ingredients. He used mud, pine cones, snow, stone, twigs and thorns. He also used flowers and leaves. This was, he thought, courageous – 'I think it's incredibly brave to be working with flowers and leaves and petals. But I have to: I can't edit the materials I work with. My remit is to work with nature as a whole.'

Andy Goldsworthy's art-school-trained, studio-built leaf collages of the 1980s and 1990s differ from Angus MacPhee's wild, outside creations. Goldsworthy had access to different varieties of leaf, such as maple and iris, which were unavailable to MacPhee. And Goldsworthy was interested in a heritable effect; in something which would last as long as possible, whereas MacPhee was not. So Andy Goldsworthy's gorgeous colours and patterns were often achieved by the judicious use of evergreens and dry, autumnal leaves. Angus MacPhee, living and working in the moment, was interested in the complexion of fresh summer deciduous blossoms, which faded to a uniform brown when the days shortened and the temperature fell – if by that time they had not been raked onto a bonfire and burnt.

By the 1970s most of Angus's close Uist family had died or dispersed. His oldest sister Mary Ellen and his youngest sister Peigi had both married Englishmen and moved away to live in the south. His Aunt Anna and his father Neil had long been lying in Ardivachar cemetery, at the western edge of the Iochdar machair.

But Patricia remained with her husband and her children on the croft at 52 Balgarva, and Patricia never forgot her brother. As the two middle siblings in four, Patricia and Angus had been close. Her sister Peigi said that Patricia 'would promise my father that she would bring him home'.

Patricia's daughter Eilidh Campbell knew nothing about her uncle Angus until her early teens, when a cruel joke by a South Uist schoolmate hinted at his existence.

> So I asked my mother, and she told me that Angus had been in the Faroes, and that he wasn't well after that. I think she wanted to shield us from it.
>
> Later, in the early 1980s, I was living in Inverness, and that's when I started going to visit him at Craig Dunain. My

visits were lovely. I'm not sure he knew who I was. I took along family photographs and introduced myself, and I'd chatter away to him in Gaelic, and sing to him in Gaelic, and he would just occasionally say yes or no, in English. I'd talk to him in Gaelic and he'd reply in English. Perhaps he thought I was an inspector or an official come to spy on him!

Angus was so good physically, and they'd used his energies on the farm. I'd see him at work in the big strawberry patch. He had his own private corners, surrounded by rhododendrons. He had his little tool of bent wire or fence staple, and his leaves and his pile of grass.

And he had horses. There was a beautiful chestnut horse with a white dash on its head that used to hang around the fence. It would sometimes lean over and go for the pile of grass, and Angus would tap it on the nose, as if to say, 'Get off! That's my building materials!'

I'd go in to see him, and he could be anywhere in the grounds – they'd say, 'He'll be back for his meal, he always comes in for meals.' I'd take him black bogey tobacco and a copy of the *Stornoway Gazette*. I never saw him smoke, but somebody once told me that he used the *Stornoway Gazette* for cigarette papers.

He walked in big strides, stooping slightly, with his hands behind his back. I say this because when my brother Iain went with me to visit Angus, we watched him stride back to his enclosure and Iain said, 'He walks just like the old men in Balgarva used to walk, when I was young.'

He wore his boots with coils of woven grass around them, which would work themselves loose when he walked. He was in a little enclave of his own, with his knitting and his horse. He was happy.

Angus MacPhee's sister Patricia did not live to return her brother to South Uist. She died in 1985, and the croft at 52 Balgarva was assigned to her son Iain. He in his turn married a woman from Balgarva, and like so many before them they raised their family looking over the strand to southern Benbecula.

Early in 1985 Angus MacPhee passed his 70th birthday. 'I went back with the car one time,' said Joyce Laing, 'parked my car, and there were vague words with the nurses about him getting awful old – "We think he's dementing a bit."

'I thought, well, old age, not too surprising. But I did wonder if he was dementing, because that would alter the work. So I asked to have lunch with him. We took a table to ourselves. I sat down, had a drink of orange juice or something and watched him.

'And I thought, he's not dementing. He's losing his sight. Because he never spoke, he hadn't asked for spectacles or anything. They thought, he's getting muddled and confused. But he was going blind. All the leaf things that I saved were done when he was almost blind.'

In the early 1990s Eilidh Campbell received at home a phone call from Craig Dunain Hospital. 'They said, "It's about Angus MacPhee. There's a note in his file saying his family don't want to be bothered while he's still alive. But we're going to close here, and they're going out into the community.

'"Where do you want Angus?"'

The note in Angus's file did not say that his family did not want to be bothered with him while he was alive. It said, 'In the event of death, it is the wish of his relatives that Angus should be buried in South Uist. These instructions were received on 25.9.85.'

He was still remarkably fit in 1985, still striding independently about the grounds. A swollen leg which threatened to incapacitate him was successfully operated on in 1989. But he was, as Joyce Laing had noticed, losing his sight. By the early 1990s it was noted that he was blind in his right eye and suffered severe glaucoma in his left.

In 1994 a nursing report noted that Angus MacPhee 'spends his days walking around briskly. He pulls the long grass and fashions this into ropes. He no longer makes the complicated items.'

Old age had stolen his talents, but death was cheated of its power to relocate his human frame. It was not death that returned him to South Uist. That was an accomplishment of Care in the Community.

Care in the Community was a controversial mental health policy established by the British Conservative government in its National Health Service and Community Care Act of 1990.

It was at root a cost-saving measure. Care in the Community was predicated on the fact that by the end of the twentieth century, anti-psychotic drugs were so sophisticated and strong that very few people needed to be treated and contained behind locked doors. The massive asylums inherited – in spirit if not in actual premises – from the Victorian era were therefore redundant. They could be closed down, saving the National Health Service a lot of money, and transferring the financial burden to local authorities, who were expected to provide social care and domiciliary services to the incapable.

Care in the Community was supported by the libertarian views of asylums as places of confinement and the suppression of personality and free expression that were formulated in the 1960s and 1970s and found an international audience in *One Flew Over the Cuckoo's Nest*. Care in the Community was justified by the widely held belief that ever-expanding residential mental hospitals such as Craig Dunain were not only unnecessary, they were undesirable.

'Institutional care' for schizophrenics and others was deemed to have failed on two levels. It had evidently abandoned its mission to cure. In the hundred years between 1864 and 1964, the population of Craig Dunain had risen from 200 to over 1,000 patients, while the population of its catchment area had fallen. And, it was argued, mental health hospitals had contributed to the problems they were supposed to ease by institutionalising men and women to the extent that generations of the afflicted had become entirely dependent on 24-hour, year-round service and attention. That had apparently resulted in the depression of levels of expectation. Mental patients were not all expected to hold down a job for a day, but most of them were expected to be able to boil a kettle and occasionally pull bedsheets into order.

In the words of American advocates of this argument, residential mental hospitals had created 'dependency, hopelessness' and their residents had 'learned helplessness, and other maladaptive behaviors'. 'Deinstitutionalisation', replacing long-stay psychiatric hospitals with community mental health services, was proposed as the answer.

The opponents of Care in the Community argued that its image of residential mental patients as spoiled little aristocrats who had been taught to depend upon a posse of servants to perform the smallest chore was misleading. They protested that the policy gambled with the lives of vulnerable people. Rather than turn into useful citizens and become respected members of the community, they said, left to their own devices many severe schizophrenics would forget or refuse to take their medication. They would easily turn to other drugs, would become homeless, would beg, would assault and be assaulted, would steal and be stolen from, and could kill themselves and others.

Those critics were right. The first years of Care in the Community were marked by a notable increase of homeless people and beggars on the streets of British cities. In a few well-publicised incidents, recently released young schizophrenic men killed strangers. In many more unpublicised incidents, recently released young schizophrenic people killed themselves. Care in the Community, wrote Patrick Cockburn, 'must be one of the most deceptive and hypocritical phrases ever devised by a government'.

Too few people realised, before the passage of the Community Care Act in 1990, that the abandonment of the vilified Victorian asylums without an effective replacement did not represent progressive reform, but rather signalled a return to pre-Victorian standards of care. 'Prisonlike many of the old asylums may have been,' wrote Cockburn, 'but at least they were a haven for people too mentally ill to find work, food, and shelter for themselves. Inside their walls, life may have been institutionalised, but one could safely behave bizarrely or even madly without derision or persecution.'

But most of the suffering caused by Care in the Community was inflicted on people, particularly younger people, in the urban centres of Britain. An old soldier from South Uist who had spent 50 years in a Highland institution was always likely to be offered alternative care, even if it was not quite 'care in the community'. In the early 1990s the staff of Craig Dunain Hospital, agitated by approaching closure, looked for a new home for Angus MacPhee.

They hit at first upon the possibility of sending him to a care home in the town of Stornoway on the island of Lewis. To an eastern-Highland mentality, that was justified on a couple of levels. Like South Uist, Lewis was a Hebridean island full of

Gaelic speakers, where an elderly Gaelic-speaking Hebridean would presumably feel at home.

By the 1990s Stornoway had also become the headquarters of the local islands' Health Board, which covered the Uists. When Angus MacPhee was admitted to Inverness District Asylum on the last day of 1946, South Uist was part of Inverness-shire. People from the Uists were therefore subjects of the county seat in Inverness. In 1975 that ceased to be the case. A new Western Isles local authority was created to administer the 11 populated islands between Lewis and Barra Head, including the Uists. Subsequently a Western Isles Health Board was also formed, to administer the National Health Service in the same chain of islands. By the early 1990s Angus MacPhee of Balgarva in South Uist, whose health had in 1946 been indisputably the responsibility of Inverness, was technically a dependant of Stornoway.

Those bureaucratic niceties failed to take account of the fact that to almost any Uist man or woman of Angus MacPhee's generation, Stornoway was a foreign place. Their fishermen might have occasionally put in there, but everybody else in Uist looked east to Skye or south to the mainland. They did not look north to Lewis. Stornoway itself was as different from Iochdar as any other industrious Protestant Scottish burgh was from the placid Roman Catholic croftlands of South Uist. His sister Peigi, his nephew Iain and his niece Eilidh wrote to Craig Dunain protesting vehemently against any proposal to post their brother and uncle to Lewis.

Their appeal was successful. A place was found for Angus MacPhee at Uist House in Daliburgh.

The small township of Daliburgh was 20 miles due south of Iochdar, but it was in South Uist. It was the seat of the first hospital to be raised in the island. The Hospital of the Sacred Heart was funded by the Marquess of Bute and was built in the early 1890s by Iain 'Clachair' Campbell, the Uist stonemason whom Margaret Fay Shaw had photographed 40 years later in his retirement, expertly weaving coils of heather rope outside his cottage door. The old four-square premises built by Iain 'Clachair' was still standing firm in the 1990s. Operated for almost a century by nuns, it had been adopted, modernised and extended by the National Health Service and included a small care home for two dozen elderly people, that was named Uist House.

Early in 1996, in his 81st year and after half a century in Craig Dunain Hospital, Angus MacPhee was driven through Inverness to Dalcross Airport ten miles east of the town.

When he had arrived from the west 50 years earlier, Inverness was a sleepy country burgh with some 25,000 people huddled together on the hillsides and floodplain east and west of its broad eponymous river. In 1996 the town's population was greater than 40,000, and its sprawling new suburbs contained as many people again. In 1946 Craig Dunain was some distance from the western boundaries of Inverness; by 1996 Angus MacPhee could see new housing estates crawling relentlessly across the farm's green fields towards the old asylum on the mount. Inverness in the 1990s was as raucous and neon-lit as any town in late-twentieth-century Britain. It had become home to a huge new hospital at Raigmore and the offices of a regional development agency. In 1946 Inverness and the Uists shared a similar atmosphere. By 1996 it had evaporated.

There was no civilian airport at Dalcross in 1946, only a Royal Air Force base which opened for civil purposes in 1947. By 1996 there were scheduled services from Inverness to the airport at Balivanich in Benbecula, just across the white strand from Balgarva.

Although he had left the hospital grounds on many occasions in the previous 50 years – for medical appointments in Inverness, for outings, and for an occasional seven-day vacation with other patients at Butlins Holiday Camp in Ayrshire – this was Angus MacPhee's first flight in an aeroplane. A few days before he was due to leave, an aircraft flew low over Craig Dunain. A nurse pointed to it and said, 'Soon it will be us up there. Do you feel frightened by the thought of flying?'

Angus looked at the aeroplane. Then he trembled like a circus clown. Then he laughed heartily, and strode off into the rhododendron bushes with his hands clasped behind his back.

On Monday 12 February 1996 Iain and Bella Campbell drove over the South Ford to meet him at Balivanich Airport, to take him to Uist House, and to reunite Angus MacPhee with Balgarva. 'The first day after he came back we let him go out to the garden, and he was pulling out grass,' said Iain Campbell.

> And we couldn't get him in, he wouldn't come in. He started working on grass, and he wouldn't come in at all. He was out there for three or four hours. The weather was bad at the time. It was in the winter he came over.
>
> So I pulled a lot of grass out myself and put it in a fish-box, which I used to take in every day when he came. And he just worked away with that. He would just make the plaited ropes . . . by this time he was quite blind, so he couldn't really see what he was doing, but he could feel, and he made a pair of shoes. But they didn't look very much like shoes because he was so blind, he couldn't see what he was doing, he was just feeling what he was doing.
>
> I was asking Peigi where he would have learned the grass-weaving from, and she reckoned they used to do the horse's

halters from marram grass, and they would weave that, and that's the only thing Peigi could think he got it from. That's the only thing she could think of that they would be making.

He knew where he was. He knew he was back home. He recognised the house further down. He said 'Tigh Niall Ruadh!' – that was the people who lived there when he was here. And he went over to the old house over there, the old thatched house where he was brought up, and stood by it and kept tapping the wall, and the thatch. I'd put a bit of rope around to hold the thatch down rather than stones, some heavy rope from the shore, and he was very fascinated with that, kept touching it all the time, wondering what it was.

I used to bring him down here to Balgarva every second weekend from Uist House in Daliburgh. I used to work every other weekend, so the weekend I was off I used to take him down, to see myself and my wife and Peigi, who had moved back up here from England after her husband died.

He was definitely happy, being back in Uist. I visited him a couple of times in Craig Dunain, and he was very much quieter there. He wouldn't say much in Craig Dunain. But if you mentioned people that lived in Balgarva, you could tell that he ... he started smiling when you mentioned their names. But very little else. But back in Uist ...

I went to collect him from Uist House one day and one of the nurses said to him in Gaelic, 'Where are you going, Angus?' And he said, in Gaelic, 'To a proper place ...' meaning he was coming here, to Balgarva!

Yes, he was all right. Very quiet. He wouldn't make a conversation with you at all – he would answer questions, in Gaelic mostly. He was all right with English too though ... But he wouldn't make much of a conversation. He would just answer your question, and that would be it. But even as a youngster he was very quiet.

Angus MacPhee had deposited a lot of goodwill and affection in 50 years on the high hill outside Inverness. Five days after his return to Uist a nurse from Craig Dunain telephoned to ask how he was. 'Staff [at Uist House] are beginning to see an improvement in Angus over last two days,' she noted. 'Is forming relationships with two other residents who knew him as a young man. Staff have suggested I prepare a cassette tape for Angus instead of sending him a letter.'

Four days after that she telephoned Uist again. 'Angus is settling well,' she reported happily, 'and finding his way around the home. Continues his friendship with fellow residents Ronald and Alastair.'

While she was living in England, Peigi Cross, née MacPhee, had regularly visited her sister's family on the croft at 52 Balgarva. She continued the visits after Patricia's death, and eventually retired to an annex at the back of Iain and Bella Campbell's modern bungalow, the latest addition to the cluster of several generations of housing by the sea at the foot of the croft.

'We had a phone call saying they was going to bring Angus home,' Peigi told the film-maker Nick Higgins in 2004. 'We never thought that he would outlive Pat. She was two-and-a-half years younger, Patricia, you know, his sister.'

'How was it when he came back here at the end, then?' asked Higgins.

'He was wonderfully well.'

'Did he talk to you at all?'

'Not a lot. Not a lot, no,' said Peigi. 'You couldn't make a lot of conversation with him. But his life had been so remote and so different . . . now you'll have me crying and I'm not a big crier. You'll have me crying next.' She laughed lightly, sadly.

In 1996, during Angus MacPhee's first year back in South Uist, Joyce Laing planned a major touring exhibition of her

Art Extraordinary collection. 'The art people were becoming very interested in outsider art,' she said.

The tour was scheduled to travel to Aberdeen, Skye, Mull, Peebles, and to a small four-year-old museum and arts centre called Taigh Chearsabhagh at Lochmaddy in North Uist. In September it would open and run for five weeks at the Talbot Rice Gallery, the University of Edinburgh's public art gallery.

It featured most of the work which had first appeared as Art Extraordinary at the Glasgow Print Studio in 1978. Once again, the highlights were Adam Christie's enigmatic stone human faces and torsos, and the showpiece, signature garments of Angus MacPhee's surviving repertoire: the tunic, the boots, the trousers.

They were transported north-west to Uist in the spring of 1996, to be shown at Taigh Chearsabhagh. It would be the first time that Angus MacPhee's Hebridean work had breathed the Hebridean air, and the first time that the people of the Western Isles, who by then once again included Angus MacPhee, had the chance to see the celebrated expressions of an eccentric native son.

'He wouldn't go,' said Iain Campbell. 'I asked him if he would like to go over to Taigh Chearsabhagh when it was showing. He just laughed. He thought it was very, very funny that anybody would want to see his work. He couldn't understand what all the fuss was about. After all, he used to help them burn his things in the bonfires in Inverness . . . Or it would turn into compost outside in the bushes . . .'

Before the exhibitions opened, in the early summer of 1996 Joyce Laing travelled to Daliburgh with the writer and photographer Tim Neat to visit Angus MacPhee in Uist House. She took him a variety of different wools, 'and he eagerly felt each strand with his fingers.' She told him of the planned Talbot Rice and Taigh Chearsabhagh exhibitions. 'Angus was a man who had come home,' she wrote later, 'and his whole being reflected his happiness.'

Tim Neat mentioned the photograph which had been taken in 1939, of Angus on horseback in his Lovat Scouts battledress. Angus MacPhee smiled. 'Aye,' he said, 'he was a fine gelding.'

It was the first time that Joyce Laing had heard him speak. It would be the last time that she heard him speak.

Angus MacPhee died of a heart attack in Uist House shortly before nine o'clock on the morning of Tuesday 11 March 1997. He had passed his 82nd birthday two months earlier. The man who loved Uist to distraction had spent just 24 of those 82 years in the Western Isles.

He would spend eternity in the island. Angus MacPhee was buried two miles from Balgarva behind the low stone walls of Ardivachar cemetery, where a spit of green land nudges into the Atlantic Ocean on the westernmost edge of Iochdar machair. A modest headstone was placed on his grave. It was inscribed: 'In Loving Memory of Angus Joseph MacPhee, 52 Balgarva. *Fois agus Sith.* [Rest and Peace.]'

On the dunes beyond the walls of the cemetery clumps of marram grass bent in the wind, the sea crashed on the sand, and the grazed turf muffled the faraway sound of horses' hooves.

7

ANOTHER AGE

～ *'They saw in the rainbow the still bent bow of a god thrown down in his negligence; they heard in the thunder the sound of his beaten water-jar, or the tumult of his chariot wheels; and when a sudden flight of wild duck, or of crows, passed over their heads, they thought they were gazing at the dead hastening to their rest.'* ～

'Inner Necessity', the Talbot Rice Gallery's exhibition of the work of Angus MacPhee and other outsider artists, had opened in Edinburgh on 28 September 1996. The title of the display was taken from the Russian abstract artist Wassily Kandinsky's term for his personal devotion to 'fervour of spirit and deep spiritual desire'.

'It is part of the mission of the Talbot Rice Gallery,' wrote its curator Duncan Macmillan in a courageously British attempt to engage with the Gallic philosophy of Jean Dubuffet,

to endeavour to look at art, not simply as a manifestation of taste, whatever that may be, but in the context of the kind of wider intellectual and imaginative endeavour that a university represents.

This involves asking the question, how does art work? What purpose does it serve? How is it part of the way we know the world? What does it mean to be 'creative'? This exhibition explores those questions at a point where they are most highly focussed, the experience of those who, through the misfortune of mental illness, live at the edge, or even beyond the edge of the order that most of us take for granted in the world, even if sometimes we have to struggle to maintain it.

Professor Henry Walton, Edinburgh University's Emeritus Professor of Psychiatry, introduced the exhibition catalogue by asking, 'Is creativity sometimes liberated by illness and adversity? Can psychic disintegration be kept at bay by art? . . . Dubuffet was the first to say this unofficial art was immediate in a way the "art of the museums" was not. Dull would he be of soul who could stand before the scratched sculpture of Adam the Shetlander, or the grass garments of Angus MacPhee, without renewed respect for the human spirit.'

A reviewer for the *Guardian* newspaper had earlier visited the 'Inner Necessity' exhibition when it was showing in Aberdeen. 'An exhibition of the work of Angus MacPhee was on display,' she wrote later. 'I had never heard of him . . .'

There were boots – fragile, woven in grass; a vest – perfectly netted together with commas of sheep wool, caught on fences, taken and spun by Angus between his fingers. And sandals – a cushion of beech leaves embellished with a strap of twisted grass. There were hats – wide-brimmed sunhats and others in the Davy Crockett style; there were leads and harnesses for ponies, socks, waders and jumpers. All at once they seemed simple, complex, pointless, glorious . . . It is difficult to say what Angus MacPhee's work showed me, but I am richer for having seen it.

Donnie Munro, the Skye musician and lead singer of the Gaelic rock band Runrig, was an alumnus of Gray's School of Art in Aberdeen. As a young arts graduate Munro worked in the Royal Edinburgh Psychiatric Hospital and the Andrew Duncan Clinic, which was established in 1965 and named in tribute to an eighteenth-century medical reformer and founder of the Edinburgh Lunatic Asylum.

There, said Munro, 'I could see at first hand the benefits of enabling expression through a visual medium. I have always felt that the arts offer a level playing field, where all artists, at whatever level of education, training, rawness, naivety or sophistication they operate, work to give full expression to their own individual "special needs". Therefore the boundaries of art are much more diffuse than we might care to imagine.'

In the early 1990s Donnie Munro was elected Rector of Edinburgh University. 'At that time,' he said, 'I first came into contact with Joyce Laing. I had links with the Talbot Rice Centre, and some knowledge of the art and music therapy work which was taking place through Edinburgh University Settlement – the social action centre that works for disabled and disadvantaged individuals.'

So it was that this famous Gaelic singer first saw Angus MacPhee's work when it was exhibited in Edinburgh.

I walked into the main exhibition area in the company of Joyce Laing and was confronted by these incredible creations suspended in glass cases like a surreal archaeological find.

They were, indeed, as something of an archaeological revelation, like artefacts from another age, the intricately woven garments uniquely fashioned using rough grass, wool and beech leaves to create human garments of mythological proportions.

Angus MacPhee created, said Munro,

> out of the natural found materials, work of incredible intricacy and power, the techniques which would have been learned in his Uist boyhood surfacing like an archaeology of the mind, a point of contact, a realism of nature, amidst the uncertain truth of mental illness.
>
> The objects were in themselves visually powerful as they invited enquiry, searching and a sense of wonderment at some greater space, a world where the ordinary was elevated to greatness . . .
>
> Angus MacPhee's work is a powerful evocation of a world which, in his life, was fast disappearing, the love for the horse, the rough rope, the harness, the mythology of the gigantic heroes of a Celtic past, the powerful omnipresence of man and nature locked in struggle and permanent partnership.

There is filmed footage of people looking at Angus MacPhee's woven objects. Their faces suggest that most of them share Donnie Munro's wonderment. Their first response is to stop still and gape. Their second response is recognition, at which point they smile knowingly, often secretly to themselves. Their third is to examine and admire.

The main garments – the tunic, the trousers, the boots – can only be appreciated in person, in real time. Still or moving film does not pass on their power. The sheer size of them is compelling. Baggy and misshapen with the passing of the years, they nonetheless convey a strange conviction. They are unmistakably what they are – a tunic, trousers, a pair of boots – but equally obviously not those things. Tunics are made from wool, trousers from cloth, boots from leather. Outside the extraordinary world of Angus MacPhee, none of them are made from woven grass to fit a well-proportioned eight-foot man.

If they first provoke the question of what on earth they are, which is relatively quickly answered, they secondly insist that the viewer discovers how they were made. That takes more time, and is full of surprises. Finally and most lastingly, they make the watcher wonder why. There is no single answer to the final riddle. Their creator made them because he needed to make them. They fell into his head from the sky, and he could not relax until they had been given form. We know where they came from. They came from an ancestral tradition of weaving marram grass and heather. But we do not know where they were going, and neither apparently did Angus MacPhee. He was occupying and amusing himself. If he incidentally amused and intrigued you too, he was an unassuming man who had no objection to that.

The art establishment is equally uncertain – almost as uncertain as was Angus MacPhee – about the status of his work. It is still argued that unconscious art cannot be art; that art may only be created by an artist who sets out to make art. Angus MacPhee proves that to be a dubious assertion. Angus MacPhee might not have called his discipline art, and certainly placed no material value on it, but he knew what he was doing. He plucked grass, flowers and leaves deliberately, to make them into tunics, hats, sandals or swallow-tailed coats. As they were not made for exhibition – as they were entirely disposable – they were never given the polish of a professional. His leaf creations are unlike the leaf creations of Andy Goldsworthy partly because they have faded, and partly because they are not addressed to a gallery audience. In skill, craft and imagination they are equal.

They are at least equal. Angus MacPhee had natural artistic ability and artistic vision, or the terms have no meaning. He was not trained by an art school to finish and treasure his work, and he operated out of doors in the grounds of a Highland mental hospital rather than in a studio. He had only his fingers and a piece of fence wire, some snagged wool, leaves and grass, but he worked as best as he could for 50 years.

His own opinion of what he did is interesting, but should not define it. Others are allowed to make their own judgements. If we are free to recognise as being dreadful much of the art which is self-consciously created by people who call themselves artists, the converse is possible. Good art may be created by somebody who never thought of himself as an artist, not least because his sense of self was shattered by illness. He will not give us neat and pretty work. As Jean Dubuffet said, he will give us raw art.

Three years later, in 2000, Angus MacPhee's objects were exhibited again at Taigh Chearsabhagh in North Uist. 'Many people of Angus MacPhee's generation,' said the gallery's manager, a North Uist man called Norman MacLeod, 'who came from a crofting and fishing background in the islands were able to weave grass with their hands. What makes Angus extraordinary is the question of what went on inside his mind when he created these works of art, and why he created them.

'They baffle some people. When we had the first exhibition I had to insure the exhibition in transit from Joyce Laing. The insurance company could not get their heads around insuring grass. Eventually we came to an agreement that it was an art object and not just grass that we were insuring.'

To accompany the 2000 exhibition Taigh Chearsabhagh published a collector's item in the shape of a short, lavishly illustrated book by Joyce Laing about Angus MacPhee's work titled *Weaver of Grass*. 'Angus MacPhee,' concluded Joyce Laing, 'has become a legend of our time.'

In 2003 Joyce Laing opened her own permanent exhibition at Pittenweem in Fife. The Art Extraordinary Gallery contained the fruits of her collection since that winter's day in 1977 when, at the prompting of Tom McGrath, she had caught the train to Inverness and been told by a taxi driver that there was a man in the hospital who made things from grass. Adam Christie's stone statuettes were there, and Antonia Jabloner's many swirling shapes and colours, and Lachlan Kilmichael's psychedelic landscapes, and the innocent flora of Mrs McGilp, and the work of a score of other original and wholly unpretentious artists.

At the back of the Art Extraordinary Gallery, louring over the other exhibits like a friendly ogre, hung the work of the first and finest of them all – the polo-necked grass tunic of Angus MacPhee, in the company of his trousers, his boots, his pouches and all the other creations which Joyce Laing had succeeded in saving from the bonfires at Craig Dunain.

In 2004 the film-maker Nick Higgins, having read Joyce Laing's *Weaver of Grass*, made a haunting 25-minute documentary about 'the quiet big man from South Uist who wove clothes from grass'. It was titled *Hidden Gifts, The Mystery of Angus MacPhee* and won international acclaim. *Hidden Gifts* was nominated for a Royal Television Society Programme Award, was an Official Selection at the 14th Parnu International Documentary and Anthropology Film Festival in Estonia, was an Official Selection at the Monterey

International Film Festival in Mexico, and won the award for the Best Documentary Film at the Britspotting '05 Festival in Germany and Switzerland.

In 2006 the people of Switzerland had the chance to see Angus MacPhee's work. It was flown by Swissair to the place where it all began, to join for a short period Jean Dubuffet's seminal collection at the Collection de l'Art Brut in Lausanne. 'They did an exhibition of textiles by outsider artists,' said Joyce Laing. 'A lot of Angus's work went. The big tunic, the boots, vests, halters, pony things, satchels ... I went to the opening. Everything was of such beautiful quality. There was an amazing wedding dress made of string by a woman in a mental hospital. And when Angus's material was returned, it was so perfectly wrapped and packaged. They know what they're doing in Lausanne!'

Joyce Laing once commented that other artists, working in all media, responded viscerally to Angus MacPhee's work. In 1997 Eilidh, Fiona and Gillian MacKenzie, three sisters from the largest Hebridean island of Lewis who formed the Gaelic folk group MacKenzie, released their first album, *Camhanach*. It contained a song called 'A' Fighe le Feur' ('Knitting Grass'):

> *Buachaille o-ro, buachaille o*
> *Hi-ri-ri o hi u a hu a ho-ro*
> *Buachaille o-ro, buachaille o*
> *Hi-ri-ri o hi u a hu a ho-ro*
> *Fuaim as neonaiche na cuala sibhse riamh?*
> *Aonghas Mac-a-Phi a' fighe le feur.*
> *Figh na lion 's glac run diamhair*
> *Aonghais Mhic-a-Phi a' fighe le feur.*
> *Le bioran 'fas nas maoil' is d'inntinn 'fas nas geur'*
> *Aonghais Mhic-a-Phi a' fighe le feur.*

Sealladh as boidhche na chunna sibhse riamh?
Aonghas Mac-a-Phi a' fighe le feur.

(Have you ever heard a stranger sound
Than Angus MacPhee knitting with grass?
Weave the web and trap your secret purpose
O Angus MacPhee knitting with grass.
With your needles growing blunter and your mind
  growing sharper
O Angus MacPhee knitting with grass.
Have you ever seen a more beautiful sight
Than Angus MacPhee knitting with grass?)

In 1998 the Scottish poet Brian Johnstone wrote the following poem inspired by the life and work of Angus MacPhee, to whom the poem is dedicated. It was subsequently published in *Edinburgh Review*.

Outsider

These were his ordinary shoes,
this his ordinary vest, this shirt
he could have worn this rough
and fibrous on his skin, each
woven blade, each seed head, stalk,
each thread of root replacing loss
with need. You realise it was his life.
No measure could exist to take
that sleight of hand from fingers
that had known it, such as these.
And these his ropes twined;
seasons, days and hours sown in
like bits of leaf or bark, their spirits
stitched about him, worn until

he laid them on the ground.
This ordinary creel, that harness
hanging by the wall, each one
an offering, an ordinary thing
from hands that plead, insist
they have none else to give.

And give this ordinary gift.

In 2004 Donnie Munro, who had by then left Runrig to pursue a solo career, released his own song, 'The Weaver of Grass':

They took him here from another place
Where the machair's sweet winds fold upon the face.
Silent turmoil rolls across his eyes.
A changing world, a troubled heart
The spirit's freedom broken from the start,
Youth forever lost in Europe's lies,
The weaver of grass is coming home.

A young man's frame with an old man's hope,
The painful journey, the turning of the rope,
Bound, forever tied to childhood's dreams.
The Lovat days now in the past,
The mounted pride that was never meant to last,
In a warring world where women sighed.
The weaver of grass is coming home.

The wind blows cold on the Black Isle's fields,
This silent world where he touches what he feels,
Held forever still on the outer line.
The darkened room, a night of sighs,
The world defined by the regimented minds,
Oh for the coloured nights of a Uist sky.
The weaver of grass is coming home

The hands still turn a desperate weave,
To search the freedoms of the open field,
Where nature's healing measure finds its way.
By the hanging tree and the windblown fence,
His darkened eyes turned inward in defence
Of a world that only he could ever dream.
The weaver of grass is coming home

The homeward road, the familiar shore,
The peewit's cry that will cry forever more.
Down through a people's line he was sure had gone,
And in this drift of a world unchanged
His weave is strengthened in the passing of his days,
So late we came to see him in his pride.
The weaver of grass is coming home.

'On one occasion,' said Munro, 'while I was introducing the background to the song at a live show in Aberdeen, a voice rang out from the depth of the audience shouting "He was my uncle!" Unfortunately, I never got the opportunity to meet up with the source of that cry.'

Craig Dunain Hospital was closed down at the very end of the twentieth century, after 136 years of operation. In 1999 and 2000 the Highland artist John McNaught was commissioned to produce a published visual archive to mark the end of the institution. 'The book uses 12 stories or anecdotes and uses linocut to illustrate, all printed on Japanese paper,' said McNaught.

It was called 'Mind Your Head', after a sign above a low door just inside the entrance to Craig Dunain. It was an amazing experience to have access to the building in its final year. We were interested in the effects of the closure on the Highland community, and the archive was as much about the culture of the Craig as it was hard facts. The written archive was produced by a nurse, Jim Neville, with artwork by myself, and photos by Craig MacKay. Our archive project was featured as part of a Gaelic TV programme in 2001.

I did one print about Angus MacPhee, and this was about his apparent understanding or 'way' with animals. He is said to have calmed a rampaging bull in the grounds of the hospital. The print was called 'Brothers in Grass', as both Angus and the bull in their different ways had an interest in the grass.

Recently, I was asked to do some work on the history of the hospital with Muirtown Primary School, who have some community woodland just above the Craig. One of the images was about Angus and we were able to use a pair of his knitted boots, which the children were fascinated by . . .

Early in 2011 another artist named Mike Inglis was commissioned by Highland Council to paint a large mural on a retaining wall in the old centre of Inverness. 'Some of the designs [in the mural] were influenced by items woven from grass and leaves by former Lovat Scout Angus MacPhee,' reported the BBC. 'Textures and patterns in the wall art were inspired by Mr MacPhee's weaving.'

'Scotland is so slow,' said Joyce Laing in the Art Extraordinary Gallery at Pittenweem. 'It took them 60 years to appreciate Charles Rennie Mackintosh. They'll discover Angus MacPhee, in time . . .'

In a corner of the Art Extraordinary Gallery there is on permanent display an assortment of sea-shells from South Uist.

Anybody who in the 1970s turned into Iochdar from the main Uist arterial road was almost immediately confronted by an astonishing apparition. On the left-hand side of the township road, a few yards from the old school which Angus MacPhee had attended, stood a small thatched crofthouse and an old motorbus. Both of them were covered with a complex mosaic of sea-shells.

They glittered in the sun. They were a fantasy brought to life, like a fairy coach and palace in the practical Iochdar crofting landscape. They were the work of Mrs Flora Johnstone. Their provenance and context were as curious as their appearance.

Metal machinery and motor engines were late arriving in the Hebrides, but once they got there, they stayed there. The same transport difficulties that delayed their appearance, and prolonged the life of the island horse culture, meant that machines had exceptional importance. The fact that until 1964 there was no car ferry to any port in the Uists led to those cars, buses, tractors, ploughs and harrows which did get hauled and hoisted from the decks of ships onto an island pier being treasured and hoarded, reconstituted and recycled well beyond the term of their natural lives.

A combination of crofter thrift and the bald fact that there was nowhere to send broken tractors, cars and machinery – who was going to pay to put a wrecked Morris Minor back on the ferry to Oban? – led to almost every croft having its own small scrapyard, and to some crofts becoming small scrapyards. When tourists from the south began slowly to discover the Western Isles in the second half of the twentieth century, they were frequently appalled and almost always surprised by the quantity of rusted metal that the inhabitants left lying, apparently heedlessly, about the primeval countryside. The rear end of cars stuck out of peat bogs; dilapidated whole cars were used as hen houses; lorry axles lay in ditches; corroded drive shafts leaned against megalithic standing stones; 1930s motorcycles were terminally parked in the shelter of Pictish brochs. In the twenty-first century the architecture critic Jonathan Meades celebrated those features of Hebridean life in a documentary called *Island of Rust*. Meades recognised that the rust was there from necessity rather than aesthetic preference, but he suggested that it had achieved a kind of rough integrity as landscape art.

So it was that Mrs Flora Johnstone came by her omnibus. It was a simple little 1950s single-decker country bus with a streamlined Art Deco front and room inside for perhaps 20 or 30 passengers. It had probably served its time on the arterial road, motoring dutifully up and down from the south of South Uist to the north of Benbecula until some fatal mechanical failure occurred, or until the new car ferry brought a superior model which forced it into early retirement.

For time-honoured reasons the little country bus would not be returned to the mainland, and there was no scrap-metal merchant in the Uists. It had to be found a new home, and hopefully a new purpose. The Iochdar crofthouse of Lachlan and Flora Johnstone was small. They adopted the redundant bus and parked it next to their home, where it was converted into an extra room. There was a symmetry to that: when the couple married in Glasgow in 1925, Lachlan had been working as a tramcar conductor.

Lachlan Johnstone died in 1968. As their children grew up and went away, Flora Johnstone found that she had less use for the extra room in the bus on the croft. She turned it into a greenhouse. Before long the inside of the old bus was a riot of herbiage. But the exterior paintwork and aluminium flashing were showing their age. It was beyond the inclination or ability of Flora Johnstone to give the bus a respray, so she hit upon an alternative. She collected sea-shells from the shore – all sizes and varieties of shells, but chiefly the ubiquitous cockles and whelks – and glued them in circular patterns to the inside of large tin lids.

She then glued the tin lids, sea-shells outwards, onto the outside walls of the bus. Before long, hundreds of sea-shell tesserae covered the bus from roof to mud-guards. The windows full of greenery were bordered with smaller shells. Flora Johnstone had created a magic bus.

Then she moved onto her house. The stone walls of the cottage got the same treatment as the metal panels of the country bus, and within a few years it too was coated with molluscs beneath the shaggy fringes of the thatch.

Flora Johnstone made keepsakes and souvenirs from shells, which she sold to tourists who stopped to admire her house and bus. She sent the proceeds to a multiple sclerosis charity. Visitors were often invited inside the sea-shell house for a cup of tea and a chat. On one occasion, she said, she entertained a man from the Evo-Stik adhesive company who discussed featuring her work in a television advertisement.

By the end of the 1980s Flora Johnstone's impeccable ornamental cottage and bus had deteriorated in the unforgiving Hebridean climate. By the twenty-first century the shell-lids had fallen off or been removed from the walls of the house, leaving only shadowy circular traces of their glorious past. The bus was hauled away, leaving only a few flakes of rust behind in Iochdar. All that could be exhibited of Flora Johnstone's transient accomplishment were some surviving shell-covered lids, a few of her charity souvenirs and a handful of photographs.

She had no mental illness whatsoever. Equally certainly, Flora Johnstone had, like Angus MacPhee, created an unforgettable form of raw sculpture which unconsciously or otherwise echoed features of Uist life. Shellfish from the shore had been part of the starvation diet of the Hebrides during famine years. The arrival of the internal combustion engine concurred with the end of true penury in the islands. If the work of Angus MacPhee celebrated the old, that of Flora Johnstone rang in the new. Neither of them intended their years of skilled and dedicated labour to deposit a permanent, let alone profitable, legacy.

It was a coincidence that they both came from Iochdar, but it was not a coincidence that they both came from South Uist. They were among the last practitioners of a demotic Celtic art which, if it was to be found anywhere in the twentieth century, would be found on that island.

Celtic fantasy, and the art that it produced, were rooted in the patterns and cycles of the natural world. The Celtic imagination wrestled with the infinite implausibilities of life. The Celtic ascendency of Roman and pre-Roman Britain, whose metalwork, illustrations and sculptures have become regarded as their islands' most sublime contribution to the art of the world, dealt chiefly in abstractions. They were more than capable of representative art, but representative art did not adequately illuminate their vision. They were too mysterious for the modern world, and sometimes too mysterious for their own good.

'You must not laugh at us Celts,' wrote the Breton philosopher Ernest Renan in 1883.

We shall never build a Parthenon, for we have not the marble; but we are skilled in reading the heart and soul; we have a secret of our own for inserting the probe; we bury our hands in the entrails of a man, and, like the witches in Macbeth, withdraw them full of the secrets of infinity. The great secret of our art is that we can make our very failing appear attractive. The Breton race has in its heart an everlasting source of folly...

It is impossible to give an idea of how much goodness and even politeness and gentle manners there is in these ancient Celts... The unselfishness and the practical incapacity of these good people were beyond conception. One proof of their nobility was that whenever they attempted to engage in any commercial business they were defrauded. Never in the world's history did people ruin themselves with a lighter or more careless heart, keeping up a running fire of paradox and quips. Never in the world were the laws of common sense and sound economy more joyously trodden under foot.

The Celtic race, said Renan, 'has worn itself out in mistaking dreams for realities.'

'Balance, measure, and patience,' the sensible English writer Matthew Arnold had proposed to Renan,

these are the eternal conditions, even supposing the happiest temperament to start with, of high success; and balance, measure, and patience are just what the Celt has never had.

Even in the world of spiritual creation, he has never, in spite of his admirable gifts of quick perception and warm emotion, succeeded perfectly, because he never has had steadiness, patience, sanity enough to comply with the conditions under which alone can expression be perfectly given to the finest perceptions and emotions.

The Greek has the same perceptive, emotional temperament as the Celt; but he adds to this temperament the sense of measure; hence his admirable success in the plastic arts, in which the Celtic genius, with its chafing against the despotism of fact, its perpetual straining after mere emotion, has accomplished nothing.

In the comparatively petty art of ornamentation, in rings, brooches, crosiers, relic-cases, and so on, he has done just enough to show his delicacy of taste, his happy temperament; but the grand difficulties of painting and sculpture, the prolonged dealings of spirit with matter, he has never had patience for.

Responding in 1897 to both Renan and Arnold, the Irish poet William Butler Yeats wrote:

Once every people in the world believed that trees were divine, and could take a human or grotesque shape and dance among the shadows; and that deer, and ravens and foxes, and wolves and bears, and clouds and pools, almost all things under the sun and moon, and the sun and moon, were not less divine and changeable.

They saw in the rainbow the still bent bow of a god thrown down in his negligence; they heard in the thunder the sound of his beaten water-jar, or the tumult of his chariot wheels; and when a sudden flight of wild duck, or of crows, passed over their heads, they thought they were gazing at the dead hastening to their rest; while they dreamed of so great a mystery in little things that they believed the waving of a hand, or of a sacred bough, enough to trouble far-off hearts, or hood the moon with darkness.

Quoting the medieval Welsh legends of the Mabinogion, Yeats drew closer to the world and work of Angus MacPhee: "'They took the blossoms of the oak, and the blossoms of the broom, and the blossoms of the meadow-sweet, and produced from them a maiden the fairest and most graceful that man ever saw; and they baptized her, and called her Flower Aspect"; and one finds it in the not less beautiful passage about the burning Tree, that has half its beauty from calling up a fancy of leaves so living and beautiful, they can be of no less living and beautiful a thing than flame.'

163

The people who came to share the British Isles with the Celts, who pushed those wanderers to the western seaboard and islands of the archipelago, who produced artists such as William Shakespeare and John Keats – those people also regarded the natural world, said W.B. Yeats. But 'they looked at nature without ecstasy, but with the affection a man feels for the garden where he has walked daily and thought pleasant thoughts.

'They looked at nature in the modern way, the way of people who are poetical, but are more interested in one another than in a nature which has faded to be but friendly and pleasant, the way of people who have forgotten the ancient religion.'

Renan, Arnold and Yeats were agreed upon at least one indisputable fact. Celts were not classical Greeks or Romans. Whatever their respective merits, Celtic art was not part of the representative Graeco-Roman tradition which for two millennia monopolised European culture even within the old Celtic territories. Regardless of the mental condition of its creators, Celtic art was antithetical to the classical ethos from which Jean Dubuffet and scores of his illustrious contemporaries struggled to extract themselves. Celtic art had its disciplines, its measure and its balance, but they were not strictures. They did not dictate the form; they were subordinate to the form. Celtic art derived from a less sensible and unregimented human reverie. It honoured the colours and shapes of dreams.

However Angus MacPhee viewed the wind and rain, the sun and racing clouds, the tumultuous ocean, the bent grass, the leaves and the small, brave flowers of his surroundings, it was not with 'the affection a man feels for the garden where he has . . . thought pleasant thoughts'. His instincts, and those of his perennially independent people, were impulsive, witty, inventive and frequently fantastic.

He was out of his time in the second half of the twentieth century, but he won back the past. He translated vegetation that had flourished in the Highlands of Scotland before any human civilisation into cultural artefacts which by his lifetime were manufactured mainly from rubber, leather, plastic, metal and artificial fibres. His motives for making his burning tree were unfathomable, but make it and burn it he did.

It cannot be known if he was the first Celt in Europe to construct a pair of laced boots from woven grass and a pair of sandals from leaves. It can fairly be assumed that he was the last.

NOTES

CHAPTER ONE
THE HORSE SOLDIERS

p. 1   'Two people from that house . . . They all loved going.' Peigi Cross, née MacPhee, in the documentary film *Hidden Gifts*, directed by Nick Higgins, 2004

p. 2   'It was the best way for getting a fortnight's holiday . . . and had a good time.' *Polly*, Roger Hutchinson, Edinburgh, 1990

p. 3   'The horses in Iochdar were famous . . . depended on them.' Fr Michael J. MacDonald, email to author, 2010

p. 5   'It was demanding work . . . Gaelic song and the "mouth music" with many good tales thrown in.' *The Story of the Lovat Scouts, 1900–1980*, Michael Leslie Melville, Moray, 2004

p. 6   'But I was daft about horses . . . horse races and the like.' Interview with author, 2010

p. 6   'We used marram grass . . . and sell them in the district.' Interview with author, 2010

pp. 6–7   'In the '30s and the '20s . . . that's what my father would thatch with.' Peigi Cross, née MacPhee, in the documentary film *Hidden Gifts*, directed by Nick Higgins, 2004

p. 7   'That Friday night . . . went back and got the horse.' Interview with author, 2010

p. 8   'spent what seemed like hours . . . splashing through the water.' *The Story of the Lovat Scouts, 1900–1980*, Michael Leslie Melville, Moray, 2004

p. 11   'Chaos ruled mainly . . . killing them with our bayonets.' Unpublished memoirs of Donald John MacKenzie, edited by George Hendry, available online at http://www.scotsatwar.org.uk/veteransreminiscences/dmackenzie.htm

p. 11   'Training was carried out . . . night training, anti-gas precautions . . .' *The Story of the Lovat Scouts, 1900–1980*, Michael Leslie Melville, Moray, 2004 pp. 11–12 'Our main task for the first period . . . but soon we were very competent riders.' Unpublished memoirs of Donald John MacKenzie, edited by George Hendry, available online at http://www.scotsatwar.org.uk/veteransreminiscences/dmackenzie.htm

pp. 13–14 'the flat country . . . the Lovat Scouts' *The Story of the Lovat Scouts, 1900–1980*, Michael Leslie Melville, Moray, 2004

p. 14 'We had a feather bed . . . his dart board at the twenty and the bull.' Unpublished memoirs of Donald John MacKenzie, edited by George Hendry, available online at http://www.scotsatwar.org.uk/veteransreminiscences/dmackenzie.htm

p. 15 'We were mechanized . . . too small for me . . . We suffered . . .' Unpublished memoirs of Donald John MacKenzie, edited by George Hendry, available online at http://www.scotsatwar.org.uk/veteransreminiscences/dmackenzie.htm

pp. 17–18 'Round about the town . . . those hopeless-looking hills.' *The Atlantic Islands. A Study of the Faeroe Life and Scene*, Kenneth Williamson, London 1948

p. 18 'crowds of people . . . remained there all day.' *The Story of the Lovat Scouts, 1900–1980*, Michael Leslie Melville, Moray, 2004

pp. 19–20 'Oh, we had a great reception . . . they were friendly, oh, very very friendly.' Interview with author, 2010

p. 20 'The Faroese are hospitable . . . someone is almost sure to ask them in for cakes and coffee.' *The Northern Garrisons*, Eric Linklater, London 1941

pp. 20–21 'We took over from . . . was a very sea-worthy craft.' Unpublished memoirs of Donald John MacKenzie, edited by George Hendry, available online at http://www.scotsatwar.org.uk/veteransreminiscences/dmackenzie.htm

p. 21 'When held firm . . . with a single magazine.' *Quartered Safe Out Here*, George MacDonald Fraser, London 1992

p. 22 'Here's to . . . to do it again.' *The Story of the Lovat Scouts, 1900–1980*, Michael Leslie Melville, Moray, 2004

pp. 22–23 'was Major Richard Fleming . . . seven miles back to the billets.' Unpublished memoirs of Donald John MacKenzie, edited by George Hendry, available online at http://www.scotsatwar.org.uk/veteransreminiscences/dmackenzie.htm

p. 23 'It was a great pleasure . . . game with Tommy-guns.' *The Northern Garrisons*, Eric Linklater, London 1941

CHAPTER TWO
TIR A' MHURAIN

p. 27 'The best arable . . . been sent to inferior lands . . .' *Evidence taken by Her Majesty's Commissioners of Inquiry into the conditions of the crofters and cottars in the Highlands and Islands of Scotland*, Volume I, London, 1884

pp. 27–28 'We are yearly getting poorer . . . unproductive ground . . .' *Evidence taken by Her Majesty's Commissioners of Inquiry into the conditions of the crofters and cottars in the Highlands and Islands of Scotland*, Volume I, London, 1884

pp. 28–29 'A skilled, unmarried farmworker's . . . three and sixpence [£10.50p] a bottle . . .' *The Furrow Behind Me*, Angus MacLellan, introduced and translated from Gaelic by John Lorne Campbell, Edinburgh 1997

pp. 30–32 'There was a lad from Uist out there . . . Indeed I won't.' *The Furrow Behind Me*, Angus MacLellan, introduced and translated from Gaelic by John Lorne Campbell, Edinburgh 1997

p. 37 'When they arrived . . . nothing but Gaelic.' Interview with author, 2011

pp. 37–38 'Religion featured prominently . . . and left them bereft.' Interview with author, 2011

pp. 38–39 'The early historians of Scotland . . . and well-stocked land on the north-west.' *History of the Outer Hebrides*, W.C. MacKenzie, London 1903

p. 41 'It was a very sad, black place . . . in the early 1920s,' Author's interview with Eilidh Shaw, 2011

p. 42 'Their colonel in the Cameron Highlanders . . . as she had lost two sons in the war.' Fr Michael J MacDonald, email to author, 2011

p. 44 'the lamb marking . . . by law four times a year.' *Folksongs and Folklore of South Uist*, Margaret Fay Shaw, Oxford 1955

p. 44 'O mo dhuthaich . . . Land where everything is plentiful . . .' *Folksongs and Folklore of South Uist*, Margaret Fay Shaw, Oxford 1955 pp. 46–47 'The houseman is twisting twigs . . . where this grass grows.' *Carmina Gadelica, Ortha nan Gaidheal*, Volume One, Alexander Carmichael, Edinburgh 1900

pp. 49–50 'The natives are much addicted to riding . . . a quantity of wild carrots.' *A Description of the Western Isles of Scotland*, Martin Martin, London 1703

p. 50 'As I came from South-Uist . . . which are exceeding plentiful there.' *A Description of the Western Isles of Scotland*, Martin Martin, London 1703

pp. 50–51 'Along the road . . . as if it were not worthy of comment.' *A School in South Uist*, Frederick Rea, London 1964

p. 51 'By a curious coincidence . . . and other sports.' *Carmina Gadelica, Ortha nan Gaidheal*, Volume Two, Alexander Carmichael, Edinburgh 1900

p. 52 'At a distance of two . . . which answered equally the purpose.' Unpublished history of South Uist, by Fr Alexander Campbell

p. 54 'pretty primitive . . . good laughs, yes.' Peigi Cross, née MacPhee, in the documentary film *Hidden Gifts*, directed by Nick Higgins, 2004

pp. 54–55 'I was at school with them . . . a very nice, quietly spoken boy.' Interview with author, 2010

p. 55 'Angus was such a lover of horses . . . "How did these horses get so mild ..?"' Interview with author, 2011

p. 55 'the bobs my father . . . lost their mothers.' Peigi Cross, née MacPhee, in the documentary film *Hidden Gifts*, directed by Nick Higgins, 2004

CHAPTER THREE
THE ROCKY HILL OF THE BIRD

p. 59 'His father wanted him back . . . he would take over the croft.' Interview with author, 2011

p. 60 'He couldn't cope with it . . . He seemed unable to cope. Couldn't cope.' Peigi Cross, née MacPhee, in the documentary film *Hidden Gifts*, directed by Nick Higgins, 2004 pp. 60–61 'Nobody seems to know . . . while he was pushing it . . .' Interview with author, 2010

p. 61 'They all thought . . . I didn't see him for years.' Peigi Cross, née MacPhee, in the documentary film *Hidden Gifts*, directed by Nick Higgins, 2004

pp. 61–62 'His attack of illness . . . at the top of his voice the word "pipe".' *Craig Dunain Hospital, Inverness, One Hundred Years, 1864–1964*, Martin M. Whittet, Inverness 1964

p. 63 'He had been insane . . . twice in the course of the year.' *Report of the Royal Commission to inquire into the condition of Lunatic Asylums in Scotland, and the existing state of the law in that country in reference to Lunatics and Lunatic Asylums*, London 1857

p. 65 'has drained the Highlands and Islands . . . or among the hills.' *Craig Dunain Hospital, Inverness, One Hundred Years, 1864–1964*, Martin M. Whittet, Inverness 1964

p. 67 'The dread of the Asylum . . . attached to such a move.' *Craig Dunain Hospital, Inverness, One Hundred Years, 1864–1964*, Martin M. Whittet, Inverness 1964

pp. 71–72 'Almost all schizophrenics paint . . . And they'd be away . . .' Interview with the author, 2011

p. 72 'the genetic inheritance . . . original and creative minds.' *Henry's Demons*, Patrick and Henry Cockburn, London 2011

p. 73 'able, original, likeable . . . what he wanted to do himself.' *Henry's Demons*, Patrick and Henry Cockburn, London 2011

p. 73 'In this hospital . . . a shell of what they used to be.' *Hidden Gifts*, directed by Nick Higgins, 2004

p. 76 'It is conceived . . . graver error could be made.' *Craig Dunain Hospital, Inverness, One Hundred Years, 1864–1964*, Martin M. Whittet, Inverness 1964

p. 82 'Many patients unable to tolerate . . . and anti-depressant drugs.' *An introduction to physical methods of treatment in psychiatry*, William Sargant and Eliot Slater, assisted by Desmond Kelly, Edinburgh 1972

p. 83 'characterized by dramatic . . . combinations of the two.' *Encyclopaedia Britannica*, London 2011

Chapter Four
Self-Medicating

pp. 84–85 'The Highland temperament . . . the gay as well as the grave occasion.' *Craig Dunain Hospital, Inverness, One Hundred Years, 1864–1964*, Martin M. Whittet, Inverness 1964

p. 85 'the somatic and medicinal . . . tranquillisers and antidepressants.' *Craig Dunain Hospital, Inverness, One Hundred Years, 1864–1964*, Martin M. Whittet, Inverness 1964

p. 86 'great stress . . . poultry, potatoes and vegetables' *Craig Dunain Hospital, Inverness, One Hundred Years, 1864–1964*, Martin M Whittet, Inverness 1964

pp. 86–87 'He was very, very good . . . he would do it. You know, that was his style.' *Hidden Gifts*, directed by Nick Higgins, 2004

p. 88 'What is found quite frequently . . . identity - re-find it, really.' *Hidden Gifts*, directed by Nick Higgins, 2004

pp. 88–89 'He wouldn't talk to anyone . . . he would weave them. He did it, and that was that.' *Hidden Gifts*, directed by Nick Higgins, 2004

p. 89 'dark and chaotic . . . giving his drawings away.' *Henry's Demons*, Patrick and Henry Cockburn, London 2011

pp. 89–90 'He made a cap. . . . and he made gloves.' *Hidden Gifts*, directed by Nick Higgins, 2004

p. 90 'Angus was an interesting character . . . he wore them on top of welly boots.' Interview with author, 2010

p. 90 'Sometimes you would meet him . . . you just feel he's still around here.' *Hidden Gifts*, directed by Nick Higgins, 2004

p. 91 'Have you seen the way . . . together with the thinner plait.' Interview with the author, 2010

pp. 91–92 'And then it all vanished . . . we never found anything like that. But I'd have loved to . . .' Interview with the author, 2011

p. 92 'So he sat on the edge of his bed . . . the sheep marking on it – it gave a punch to it, you know.' Interview with the author, 2011

p. 93 'I never heard him speak . . . look straight in front of him.' Interview with the author, 2011 pp. 94–95 'preaching alternately in English . . . their appreciation of it.' *Craig Dunain Hospital, Inverness, One Hundred Years, 1864–1964*, Martin M. Whittet, Inverness 1964

pp. 95–96 'I've known him for 30 years . . . hope to carry on.' *Tacsi*, BBC television programme by MacTV, 1997

p. 96 'When I became a councillor . . . should ever have been in there.' Interview with author, 2008

p. 97 'I have never met a set of people . . . could fill up the gap without half trying.' Unpublished letter to Dr Alasdair Maclean, 1951

p. 98 'In Gaelic, the language of the Hebrides . . . ripple with the never-ceasing wind.' *Tir a' Mhurain*, photographs by Paul Strand, commentary by Basil Davidson, Leipzig 1962

Chapter Five
A Rare State of Purity

p. 104 'He always allows himself . . . almost as a spectator . . .' *Artistry of the mentally ill*, Hans Prinzhorn, Germany 1922

pp. 106–107 'I am not afraid to put forward . . . we thirst more and more each day.' *Outsider Art*, Roger Cardinal, New York 1972

p. 110 '"Look," said McGrath . . . see what we can find in a week."' Interview with Joyce Laing by author, 2011

pp. 111–116 'There were only about 12 of us . . . anywhere else in Scotland.' Interview with Joyce Laing by author, 2011

p. 117 'To some it was a legendary institution . . . never allowed to happen again and considered best forgotten.' 'Creative Arts and the Cultural Politics of Penal Reform: the early years of the Barlinnie Special Unit, 1973–1981', Mike Nellis, in *Journal of Scottish Criminal Justice Studies*, Volume 20, 2010

pp. 118–122 'We'd start at the north . . . So that was the discovery of Angus.' Interview with Joyce Laing by author, 2011

p. 125 'There was a lot of interest . . . the two exhibitions,' Interview with author, 2011

p. 125 'I was a bit worried . . . Then I knew it was safe.' Interview with author, 2011

p. 126 'Art Extraordinary refers to . . . disabled or have mental health issues.' Joyce Laing, www.artextraordinarytrust.co.uk

Chapter Six
The Reluctant Exhibitor

pp. 129–130 'I saw him work . . . "Can we help?"' Interview with Joyce Laing by author, 2011

p. 131 'He told me there . . . Craig Dunain hospital,' *Hidden Gifts*, directed by Nick Higgins, 2004

p. 131 'The farm was closed . . . he started using beech leaves . . .' Interview with Joyce Laing by author, 2011

p. 131 'He took and overlapped . . . didn't last as long as grass.' Interview with Joyce Laing by author, 2011

p. 132 'I think it's incredibly brave . . . remit is to work with nature as a whole.' *Daily Telegraph*, 2007

p. 133 'would promise my father that she would bring him home.' *Hidden Gifts*, directed by Nick Higgins, 2004

pp. 133–134 'So I asked my mother . . . his horse. He was happy.' Interview with author, 2011

p. 135 'I went back with the car . . . he was almost blind.' Interview with author, 2011

p. 135 'They said, "It's about Angus MacPhee . . . Where do you want Angus?"' Interview with author, 2011

p. 138 'must be one of the most . . . devised by a government.' *Henry's Demons*, Patrick and Henry Cockburn, London 2011

p. 138 'Prison like many of the old asylums . . . or even madly without derision or persecution.' *Henry's Demons*, Patrick and Henry Cockburn, London 2011

pp. 141–142 'The first day after he came back we let him go out . . . But even as a youngster he was very quiet.' Interview with author, 2010

p. 143 'We had a phone call . . . You'll have me crying next.' *Hidden Gifts*, directed by Nick Higgins, 2004

p. 144 'He wouldn't go . . . it would turn into compost outside in the bushes . . .' Interview with author, 2010

CHAPTER SEVEN
ANOTHER AGE

pp. 146–147 'It is part of the mission . . . to struggle to maintain it.' Inner Necessity exhibition catalogue, Edinburgh 1996

p. 147 'Is creativity sometimes liberated . . . for the human spirit.' Inner Necessity exhibition catalogue, Edinburgh 1996

pp. 147–148 'An exhibition of the work . . . but I am richer for having seen it.' Margaret McCartney, the *Guardian*, 2004

p. 148 'I could see at first hand . . . disabled and disadvantaged individuals.' Email to the author, 2011

pp. 148–149 'I walked into the main exhibition area . . . struggle and permanent partnership.' *Angus MacPhee, Weaver of Grass*, Joyce Laing, Lochmaddy 2000

p. 151 'Many people of Angus MacPhee's generation . . . not just grass that we were insuring.' Email to the author, 2011

p. 153 'They did an exhibition . . . They know what they're doing in Lausanne!' Interview with author, 2011

p. 156 'On one occasion . . . the source of that cry.' Email to the author, 2011

pp. 156–157 'The book uses 12 stories . . . which the children were fascinated by . . .' Email to the author, 2011

p. 157 'Scotland is so slow . . . discover Angus MacPhee, in time . . .' Interview with author, 2010

pp. 161–162 'You must not laugh at us Celts . . . worn itself out in mistaking dreams for realities.' *Recollections of My Youth*, Ernest Renan, Paris 1884

pp. 162–163 'Balance, measure, and patience . . . the prolonged dealings of spirit with matter, he has never had patience for.' *On the study of Celtic literature*, part IV, London 1867

pp. 163–164 'Once every people in the world . . . forgotten the ancient religion.' *The Celtic Element in Literature*, William Butler Yeats, London 1897

BIBLIOGRAPHY

Printed Sources

Arnold, Matthew *On the study of Celtic literature*, part IV, London 1867

Cardinal, Roger *Outsider Art*, New York 1972

Carmichael, Alexander *Carmina Gadelica, Ortha nan Gaidheal*, Edinburgh 1900

Cockburn, Patrick and Henry *Henry's Demons*, London 2011

Encyclopaedia Britannica, London 2011

Evidence taken by Her Majesty's Commissioners of Inquiry into the conditions of the crofters and cottars in the Highlands and Islands of Scotland, London, 1884

Fraser, George MacDonald *Quartered Safe Out Here*, London 1992

Groome's Ordnance Gazetteer of Scotland, Edinburgh 1882

Hutchinson, Roger *Polly*, Edinburgh, 1990

Inner Necessity exhibition catalogue, Edinburgh 1996

Laing, Joyce Angus MacPhee *Weaver of Grass*, Lochmaddy 2000

Lawson, Bill *Croft History, Isle of South Uist*, Volume 2, Isle of Harris 1991

Linklater, Eric *The Northern Garrisons*, London 1941

MacKenzie, W.C. *History of the Outer Hebrides*, London 1903

MacLellan, Angus *The Furrow Behind Me*, introduced and translated from Gaelic by John Lorne Campbell, Edinburgh 1997

Martin, Martin *A Description of the Western Isles of Scotland*, London 1703

Melville, Michael Leslie *The Story of the Lovat Scouts, 1900–1980*, Moray, 2004

Prinzhorn, Hans *Artistry of the mentally ill*, Germany 1922

Ragon, Michel *Dubuffet*, New York, 1959

Rea, Frederick *A School in South Uist*, London 1964

Renan, Ernest *Recollections of my Youth*, Paris 1884

Report of the Royal Commission to inquire into the condition of Lunatic Asylums in Scotland, and the existing state of the law in that country in reference to Lunatics and Lunatic Asylums, London 1857

Sargant, William and Eliot Slater, assisted by Desmond Kelly *An introduction to physical methods of treatment in psychiatry*, Edinburgh 1972

Shaw, Margaret Fay *Folksongs and Folklore of South Uist*, Oxford 1955

Shaw, Margaret Fay *From the Alleghenies to the Hebrides*, Edinburgh, 1993

Strand, Paul, commentary by Basil Davidson *Tir a' Mhurain*, Leipzig 1962

Whittet, Martin M Craig *Dunain Hospital, Inverness, One Hundred Years, 1864–1964*, Inverness 1964

Williamson, Kenneth *The Atlantic Islands. A Study of the Faeroe Life and Scene*, London 1948

Yeats, William Butler *The Celtic Element in Literature*, London 1897

OTHER MEDIA AND SOURCES

Hidden Gifts, directed by Nick Higgins, 2004

Tacsi, by MacTV, 1997

Raigmore Hospital Reference Library, Inverness

Scotland's People website - www.scotlandspeople.gov.uk

The Army Personnel Centre, MS Support Division, Historical Disclosures Section, Brown Street, Glasgow